FROM THE DARKNESS
TO THE LIGHT

FROM THE DARKNESS TO THE LIGHT

(BETWEEN A ROCK AND A HARD PLACE)

Jenny Tshibola

Library of Congress Control Number:		2010902703
ISBN:	Hardcover	978-1-4500-7726-2
	Softcover	978-1-4500-7725-5
	Ebook	978-1-4500-7727-9

This book was printed in the United States of America.

To order additional copies of this book, contact:
Xlibris Corporation
1-888-795-4274
www.Xlibris.com
Orders@Xlibris.com
73125

Thanks to everyone who helped to make this possible,
my lawyer Bill H. P. FULD

My friends who supported me through their prayers

My loving family

My best friend Athos,
Dr. MATAMBA MUJIKA MWABA

OH LORD EVERY MORNING THAT I WAKE UP I LOOK AT THE SUN RISE, I SEE THE BRIGHTNESS OF YOUR UNIQUE WORK I THANK YOU SO MUCH FOR THE AMAZING GRACE AND BLESSINGS.

I was locked behind troubles and darkness, getting through after almost 20 years it was like sitting in a very dark room where I saw a dot of light. I kept my eyes fixed on that point, hoping to see it growing. When the dot turned to be the light, it was so bright that I couldn't see the darkness anymore.

CHAPITRE I

GOLDEN PRISON

I was in the middle of my first book when suddenly I had to confront the hardship of Canadian Immigration. It was the last week of August 2008 just before going on vacation to Vancouver, I was very happy and felt that I deserved to take my vacation since I had a challenging year at my work. I still remember that day as if it was yesterday, I was still sleeping when the phone rang that morning and I was asking myself who could call so early. I was surprised, could that be my sister with whom we planed to go on vacation together? So who could that be? I picked up the phone and I heard a woman voice that was asking me to confirm my address, she had a delivery, a mail delivery for me. Could that be a special correspondence, why someone had to call before to drop the mail? Anyway I confirmed my address and that was it. Meanwhile I woke up and packed. I left the apartment for few minutes; it was enough to miss the mail lady. She left a notice asking me to go get my mail at UPS. I didn't really like this mysterious mail and I felt deep inside that something was wrong and I couldn't tell what. I drove to my sister house where we had to gather for the departure. We stopped at UPS and I picked up the mail. It was coming from Canada Immigration, I knew then that my case was denied. I have been fighting my case for 7 years and I was feeling that I was losing the battle. I have paid more than $6000.00 in lawyers, without any success. This seem to be a very juicy business for lawyers. I think somehow I was even lucky to pay that amount, some people have paid $10.000 for lawyers. It is just difficult to understand that as immigrant with low pay job, lawyers are expecting that immigrant pay for high cost services. Lawyers have been using people emotions, they have been telling me you have to do this and that if not they will deport you. They have been scaring me, I have been paying for every single paper. I was surprised that I had to pay even for my profile; a sheet of paper with my name etc . . . I was financially exhausted, all the money I could have saved went in lawyers fees. I remember that the 2nd lawyer I got called the first one to let him know that she was taking the case and really she wanted to help and she was not asking big money, oh God please forgive me. She lied, she did such a poor job and she asked more than I have paid the first lawyer. She used me for translation, business that turned bad later because when I asked her to pay for the translation, she refused to pay and told me that it was a part of the money I owe her, I was shocked and really was upset to see that the person I respected and trusted earlier, was very bad indeed. I left her office without word and never seen her again. I didn't have the strength to fight, she was the strongest in this battle; I was a poor immigrant looking for papers.

On our trip to Vancouver, I was horrible, not really like someone you could get along with and go on vacation with. I couldn't even recognize myself. I was so different, I wasn't happy at all. I was very excited for this get away, but not anymore, especially since I have got this notice from immigration. In that letter the Immigration was asking me to meet with an Immigration officer, who had an important information for me. I had to meet this officer in a week, which means that I could go on vacation and still have to be back for the appointment; I really wanted to see Vancouver. The trip from Calgary to Vancouver through Banff seems to be the paradise for me. Even though I was miserable, my eyes couldn't get off the window, the nature, the green, the Rocky Mountains were offering such a beautiful picture. We had a quick stop at Banff by the lake, I don't remember the last time I have seen such beautiful nature. The Rocky Mountains, one of God architectures, they are so gorgeous and beautiful. Amazingly the decoration made by the evergreen fir trees was above my understanding. Those trees were aligned and I wondered how people went up there on the top of the mountains and planted all those trees. We were asking ourselves to know if the Rocky Mountains forest was natural or planted by human being. The picture was very amazing; trees were aligned from the mountains base to the top. That really took my breath; we took pictures and pictures . . . Then we recall some stories of people who used to go to Vancouver to plant trees, we then understood that some people have worked very hard, to make that happened. We crossed some green/bleu rivers; I felt like the sound of blues in the air, it was so beautiful, so peaceful far away from war, far away from the town. The rare noise in that place was the music brought by the wind, and some rare birds. How come that can happen in the same world we all live in, that some places are full of peace?

In Vancouver, we visited and had a tour in the boat on the ocean; we visited the aquarium and also the millionaire/billionaire residence on the hill top of Vancouver. No way, we couldn't believe our eyes, you live in that type of mansions, and I respect you! We took some pictures in souvenir and everything was just great.

After we have spent 5 days in Vancouver enjoying our short vacation, we packed and went back to Edmonton which has been my home for 7 years. I loved Edmonton, I liked my life in Edmonton, but something was missing. The keys of many doors, I was struggling to get asylum for 7 years, really there was no way out; I was locked in a dead end where even lawyers were not of great help. During those years I had to stick to an underpay job, low level job, not much chance of getting better position since I didn't have permanent residence and I didn't go to school in Canada. I had French Education, most of my professors were from France, and even with a bachelor degree in law, I was not lucky enough to find a job corresponding to my qualifications and experience.

My life seems like being in a golden prison. My life in Canada was peaceful but I couldn't see anything great about the future, where was I going? I was trapped and there was no way to do things that a free man usually do, some stuff like traveling outside Canada, buying a house, going to school.

The next morning upon my return, I had to go to the immigration office and meet the "officer", I was shacking and had difficulty to concentrate. I wasn't myself, for the good or bad, I drove to the immigration. I was maneuvering my car in the underground public parking when suddenly I heard a boom, a sound of metal, oh no I said to myself; I hit a pole and damaged the door of the right side of my car! Then I felt deep inside that I lost my case, I had the premonition that couldn't lie. I am a type cheerful, always positive, this time there was no mistake, I couldn't be wrong.

At the immigration I asked to see the officer, I was shocked to see her, especially wearing a bullet proof vest (?) what is this, I said to myself. It wasn't the first time I was meeting her, and she never dressed like that. Why suddenly she felt that she needed to dress a bullet proof vest to meet me? Was it that she was or the immigration was treating me like a criminal? I had pity of myself, no matter how good you can be you can still be treated as terrorist or devil anytime and end up in jail or somewhere bad depending on who is dealing with your case. All my difficulties with immigration appeared to be coming from a personal conflict, it was like someone was forcing to push me out. During the hearing the DA asked me why I didn't claim asylum in USA, since USA was where I landed first. He said that I have been to law school I should have known that. Did this guy go to law school? If yes, he should have understood that the law is a vast field and Immigration Law is a branch of International law and not a part of French civil law and criminal law what I studied. And also when you fled from war, you don't have time to check what the Geneva Convention is telling you concerning the Immigration. I still remembered my hearing, the longest ever, it took 6 hours, at the end of that hearing my lawyer congratulated me by saying he was very happy, I defended myself very well. But in the back of my mind I didn't trust the translator very much, her French was more like Quebecois than French. I couldn't pay attention to what she was translating in English, and my English at that time was very fair. I was anyhow surprised that when I got the result, it was negative. So what went wrong then? When I read the judgement I noticed so many errors due to the translation. I was speaking in French and the translator was speaking Canadian French, Quebecois which is little different from the French language from France I speak. Even though it has been long time since then, there are thinks that have been mentioned that I couldn't have said. Somewhere I even found out that the judge didn't have good knowledge of what I was talking about neither the acknowledge of the region where the conflict happened, everything was mixed up. At the Immigration the officer made me sign the reception of the deportation letter. She emphasized that I had to follow the instructions if I would want to go back to Canada in the future. I left the immigration with my eyes full of tears, the sky just collapsed on my head. What am I going to do? Where was I going? I run to my office which is in the back of the immigration building, across the street. I told my boss what happened, she was very surprised and very supportive as well as all the staff. When I left the office that day, I wasn't sure if I had the strength to drive after such shock. I couldn't believe I was forced to leave everything I was trying to build behind and start again. I was expecting so much; somewhere since I was working it shouldn't be a problem, many have got their residence luckily because of their job. I somewhere thought that I could be as lucky as those people. I lived in Canada for 7 years and enjoy it while waiting for the big chance, for the American dream to be real. Leaving was like leaving a big family behind, I was close to many at work, in the community . . .

I lived all those years hoping that sooner or later I will succeed. I had some crazy propositions, friends advised me to get married, to be able to have my papers, I refused. The second lawyer even suggested that, when I looked at her with my look that was like asking what did you just say? She understood quickly what gaff she just made and then she said, no I am saying that you can do a clean, good marriage. She knew that I didn't hear from my ex in a long time, but she knew that I was not yet divorce. No, I couldn't do that. I didn't feel right to get married just for papers. Even with a failed marriage, I still believe in the marriage that brings two beautiful people in mind and full of love to commit for lifetime, I still take marriage seriously. Under pressure, I had my back against the wall when one of my many friends I knew in Edmonton came to me and said that he wanted to help, he gave me the name of one of his friend and his address outside of the town; he told me to go to see him, he will help me. The following week end I took the bus greyhound and went to meet the friend of my friend. The guy was working in the farmer town of Brooks, I felt lost in that town. I had problems breathing the stinky air, the air was full of CO_2 from livestock, I regretted that I took that risk. The friend was sharing the house with another guy, they ordered pizza that night for dinner. We didn't talk about the purpose of my visit that night. I told him somewhere that I needed to sleep if he could show me where I was going to sleep that night. He prepared his room for me and I said to myself, I hope that this guy was not crazy to think that I was an easy girl, I wanted to sleep in peace. I couldn't believe what he said after I installed myself, he asked me where he was going to sleep? I told him that there was no way that I was going to share the room with him, if he wanted his room, I was ready to leave the room and spend the night in the living room. He didn't say anything and went to sleep in the living room. Early in the morning the friend invited me to the café for the breakfast. While taking our breakfast, I said to myself that I didn't have to waste time, I didn't want to spend one more day in that village with the risk of having that guy telling me that he wanted to sleep in his bed. Then I told him what I was looking for, I was coming from his friend and I asked him if he could help and in which way. In a blink the guy told me no, he had another plan and so . . . I said thanks to him anyway, I understood him and after the breakfast it was time for me to go back to Edmonton. During my trip back to Edmonton, I got very sick in the bus, it has been freezing. I was very sick to the point I told myself, God didn't want me to do this. We are always in hurry when it comes to what we asked God, we most of the time forget that he never go away, he still there even if we don't see and don't hear. We would wish a quick change of our situation, we would wish there is not hurt, there is no suffering, there is no hunger, there is no poverty and forget that God is the Master of time and circumstances. I didn't get that waiting patiently to see the change, was a quality for my own spiritual growth. By rushing in some decision we always end up making mistakes that cost. Everything on earth has its own time and its own season, ECC 3:1

I have been kicked out after Seven years in Canada, it was too long; I was integrated and I felt like one of those who have been blessed to come to such a peaceful land. In Africa where I am from, this type of peace is utopia, and in countries like Democratic Republic of Congo or Central African Republic, people don't know how to define peace, how to define happiness. The most difficult was how to tell those with whom I shared my 7 years in Canada, all my entourage that I was leaving. I was sad, I cried for almost a month. I wasn't getting what was happening. I let my sister and family know, it was hard on them and nobody understood why it was happening. My sister was crying, I was crying. I also called my friend of 18 years Athos, and told him what was happening, he was shocked and wisely told me to start thinking at other option. And he said, that he wasn't getting that even good people could face that kind of challenge. He was like "they really refused to give you a chance to stay?" My numerous friends said that it seem to them that criminals get away with a better deal than good people and so and so . . . As a woman of faith, my faith was shaken and I couldn't tell where I was standing and what I could believe in or who I could believe in. Did God forget me? I have prayed so much for this case. I sometimes thought that with the Lord everything should be fine, everything is a success, everything is granted. I was in denial and I was like, no this didn't happen to me. I always think that if God is with me nothing negative, no failure would stand on my way. I asked myself if there are prayers that God doesn't answer and why? I was very confused and I wasn't sure that I could have the answer to all my questions at that particular moment. I was hurt and angry at the system which on one hand was looking for immigrant workers an on the other hand was getting ride of good people, I even felt like discriminated. Many things were crossing my mind, I then started asking what is God will? Did I really want to know what God will was? No, I didn't want to, my good friend, Raynaldo Baylon brought it up. I had a month from the date I got the notice to prepare myself and leave Canada. My boss Peggy told me to feel free to take my time and do the necessary to help with my case, like to contact lawyers, counselors etc . . . I appreciated very much what Peggy did for me, no this was my fight but I saw someone standing for me, doing her best for me to stay. Peggy was running for me, she was writing letters to Ministers of Foreign Affaires, of Immigrations, to the Lawyer. She told me we want you to stay, then she emphasized she said, no I personally want you to stay. Peggy was supporting me and recommending me to Canadian authority. Oh! That was very cool, that was a recognition moment, she remembered my work; I was flattered.

Whenever I could resume to the office, I took time to talk with Raynaldo, this guy is my friend, my little brother. Raynaldo is from Phillipino and I am from Congo, I don't really know what made us to be so close. We are alike in some ways, he likes jokes, I like jokes. And every time we spent together was an explosion of laugh, crazy laugh! During the lunch break we were walking to the mall which was close by and talk, laugh like crazy. Truly I was going to miss my dear friend. The way people were looking at us, was like "are you crazy? Why are you so happy? I want to know or I want to be a part of your team". Raynalodo was so crazy that he could tell me to cross the street, and as I always check the street myself, I could see that the light was still red and there was a car coming. When I asked him why he wanted me to cross since it wasn't safe? He would say, you have an insurance coverage . . . And I was like: how do you dare say that? How will I claim the benefits after I die? One time during the lunch break we went separate ways, and promise to meet at one of clothing store in the mall, I waited Raynaldo for a long time, and then when I saw him I asked him where he has been, he told me that he was looking for me among old ladies clothing lines, I laughed and then I looked at him, I said you know what "I have been looking for you among short people clothing lines". While writing these pages I spoke to him and I told him that I was still looking for a job; he told me "why didn't you do what I told you last time?" I asked him what did you tell me? He said, I told you to wear a short and high heel then walk down the street, did you forget that? I laughed as usual and I told him he was very silly. There are many jokes, that brightened my working days. Some girls in the office commented and told me I should not let Raynaldo say silly stuff to me, how could I get mad on him, they were all jokes, nothing serious. I had a capacity of getting that, people get offend for so little and forget to live happy. I was so down with this deportation news and I tried to fight by hiring a lawyer. I was trying to fight tooth and nail hoping for miracle when one day Raynaldo said to me "you are praying, you want to stay, did you ask God what is his will?" I was afraid, I didn't want to think at that question. How come God will was so different from mine? Since I have been converted this question never crossed my mind. How do I have to question God will? I was sad and really didn't want to know. What was important for me was to have my immigration case being solved, really I didn't care. But somewhere deep inside me I still remember a revelation I got long time ago in Bangui before the war started, in the revelation I was told to leave Bangui. I was not ready to do so on my own, even though it was a revelation, I was hesitant and was praying to have a clear picture of the revelation and see in what direction to do the move. To be frank the hesitation was also coming from the fact that I thought I was already settle down, I invested then there was no way to leave everything behind. We always hang to the material and have comfort in some situation and we just forget that everything has given to us by God grace. Could I just think that he provided before, he will still provide whenever and wherever? Most of the time we hear from the Lord but we just ignore that and then we forget. I should have asked him to show me the way and let myself follow his guidance since there was a revelation. I should have remembered how far I have come and wait patiently. Since he wanted me to leave Bangui he should be able to provide for me wherever I go. Why I was having such hard time? Late that day, I called my pastor and I asked him what God will is. **He told me that God will and plan for us is happiness and success in all areas of our life**. Did I get that? I didn't, I wasn't happy with what was happening. Where is the happiness in all this trouble drama? I was thrown 7 years back. This means the starting point "0", how will I make it? The last time I have been so sad was 7 years ago when a friend of mine betrayed me by saying lies against me and have favor on my back. She was someone I loved and I helped. Life is surprising, and sometimes the magnitude of ingratitude is beyond your understanding. People are killing to reach their end and they don't care. It is very unfortunate that some people like the short cut to success and they can do whatever it takes to reach their goal. This was one of my numerous disappointments in previous relations, the past that I needed to leave behind PHIL 3:13says "But this one thing I do, forgetting those things which are behind, and reaching forth unto those things which are before". This was difficult thing to do for me. Most of us like to focus on the bad past that hurt us and on the failure instead of looking to the great future that is full of hope. I needed to replace those hurt with the promise, with the joy of believing that God mercies are renewed every morning. Anyway, every morning that I wake up, it is a victorious day, because I know I can make it without trading my integrity. Because I am confident that I can overcome whatever bothered me. The problem most of us have is that while waiting instead of building trust in the Lord Jesus, we let impatience and doubt took over. We are anxious with our eyes fixed on the problem than putting our hope and trust on the one who is able and never fail. Sometimes with the ignorance of God magnitude, our problem seems bigger than the creator.

The support from my family and friends was pouring. It was so good to feel loved and to still have support when everything seems to collapse around you. Meanwhile my sister came to the apartment and saw me packing. Then she said to me "we are praying for you to stay and at the same time you are packing? Then she mentioned that I had to have a clear picture of what I was asking for and stood for it or stick to it." She was right, how many times we pray and commit our problems in God's hands, then the next minute we lose patience and refuse to wait by doing it our way. But I knew then at that time that I had to go and it was obvious that I reached the dead end road of Canadian immigration. Another good friend of mine Mary came to see me, I was very surprised, she did very good to me. She is wonderful lady and has such good heart. I was in tears all the time she spent with me. She was talking to me and trying to reinsure me that God is good and that he will still take care of me. I was very down, and to hear those words I always believed in coming from somebody else I said to myself, really I lost it. I don't think that at that moment I ceased believing or trusting God. I was just hurt and I wanted to understand what was happening and where I was going. We talked, I cried, we prayed and gave glory to the Lord. After Mary left, I was so peaceful. Prayers, my family, my friends helped me to move on. It was amazing that 3 days before I left Canada, my spirit was up and renewed, I was smiling, I was strong. Where was that strength coming from? The Lord has heard my prayer, at this point I wasn't even asking questions. I didn't know where I was going, but that peace in my mind, that insurance was enough. You know, I felt like someone falling, suddenly here were strong arms around me to stop the fall.

I moved my stuff from the apartment, and left them at my sister place. I didn't know where I was going. I was deported to US, everything was confusion and uncertainty. Somewhere it was weird and I felt like God had a special plan for me in USA. People have been deported back home, and I was deported to USA this was cool and sounds special. The eve of my departure a group of friends came to say good bye, it was amazing that I see some coming with comfort words and I was telling them with a big smile, everything is good, I am fine. Mary was also there the last day, she was surprised, I could tell; she was like oh, how you have changed? Yes I looked bright and happy, if I was made strong before I left that was for a purpose. We had a very good evening I was happy to see that support till the end, I made our favorite donut "French beignets" with tea and since then I still cherish that moment and my friendship.

I left Edmonton on the 1st of October 2008 and there was a guy from Ethiopia or Somalia who was also deported at the same time with me. We travelled from Edmonton to Vancouver by air. During the flight everything was good except the prisoner treatment we had to endure. We have been accompanied by 2 officers and during the flight we have been sitting by the window and the 2 officers were blocking our ways by sitting by the aisle. All that was funny in one way, but not really funny to my taste. As soon as we arrived in Vancouver, we have been taken in a police car, an armor vehicle that was waiting for us on the tarmac. I was scared and as my travel mate, the driver was over speeding like in the police chase. Who was he chasing, since he had us "prisoners" in the car? We were like flying. My mate and I chat a little and we all expressed our concern. Suddenly I had that somber thought "what if this car get involved in an accident or catch fire"? We have been sitting with our hands and feet cuffed, what was that? We couldn't believe that, we have been given away as worthless. Oh God, we finally made it to Blaine after 40 minutes drive. At Blaine border patrol station, my mate and I have been separated. I have been put in a very cold cell for long hours. I might have been in that room for 8 hours. I didn't know why they were still keeping me there and for so long, I was starving and freezing. I couldn't handle the cold and I asked my coat. After long hours waiting in the cold, I was submitted to the police check and serial of questionnaire, fingers print, all the police check. I didn't eat all day, I remembered that I didn't even have a breakfast that morning, the flight was a morning flight and I didn't had a chance of eating anything. I was very exhausted and my stomach was tight; questions were crossing my mind . . . where I was going from there? I wasn't sure of the issue? One thing I was sure of is that I was calm and my attitude surprised the officers. One of them, said "Madam you are so quiet and polite" how I was so calm in the middle of storm? I don't know how it happened but I was so tempered. No, Jesus in me, the peace in me was doing all that. After we have spent 8 hours at Blaine police station, my mate and I have been put back in an other armor vehicle which drove us to TACOMA Detention Center. At TACOMA Detention Center, we went separate ways. I never saw my travel mate since that day.

CHAPITRE II

TACOMA DETENTION CENTER

Tacoma Detention Center, was another torture, the first night, I waited in the cold waiting room before to be assigned in a room. The waiting room was so cold, the cement bench was cold and I was freezing. I didn't have enough chance this time to keep my coat, I was not allowed to keep any belonging. Everything I had, jewelry, my clothes, everything have been taken away.

Someone brought me a bolony sandwich around midnight, that I never touched and neglected on the side of the cement bench where I was sitting. I couldn't eat, but I asked one favor, that I took a shower before to go to bed. Around 1:00 am I was taken for medical exam in the medical section. I was so tired and somewhere some stuff happened that night, I never remember them. It could happen that sometimes I forget stuff and maybe remember them later, but this was a real black out. I couldn't remember the X Ray exam, I was like no I never been there this was not possible. But few months later I checked with the doctor who was their that night, he told me that there was no way that someone could enter the detention center without X Ray exam, he even show me where it took place. I was so amazed and surprised that my memory was shut and I couldn't remember. What happened was too much fatigue. He was right, but I was so tired that I couldn't remember. I also did a urine exam and I tried to be funny during the pregnancy test when the Dr. told me that I was not pregnant. I don't know how being so exhausted and deceived I could still keep a high spirit and joke. I laughed at the Dr. and told her that as a matter of fact I knew I was not pregnant, I didn't date in 7 years. She looked at me surprised, and I told her that if I would have told her that, she wouldn't have believed me. I just let her do her work.

After the medical check up I was escorted to my new residence, the unit B of Tacoma Detention Center, the women section where I was going to spend 5 months. My first thought was "this is a prison". I never been in a prison all my life, I never been on drug; I committed my life to fight the loyal battle of success and refused to embrace easy path of ephemeral success. Entering the unit B of Tacoma Detention Center was giving me goose bumps. All the prisons crazy stories like the "fight, bloody fight or killing", were coming to my mind. I didn't know what I was putting myself into, how my life was going to be, I surrendered. I exchanged my clothes, panty and bra with the prison uniform, panty and bra. This was very hard for me, I felt like something was taken from me. My dignity, my freedom a part of my soul, my zone of control "me" was violated etc . . . didn't I feel that same way while I was hand and feet cuffed? It was just confusing for me, this is immigration. I was like a criminal, the explanation I have got from the border patrol officer is that I entered US without valid document; really? I was brought here by Canadian Immigration, how come they have been allowed to do such think? Why American Immigration wasn't asking Canadian authorities to provide valid documents before they let me enter US? It seems like Canada refused to accept any responsibility of punishing me and was leaving this responsibility to US. I even had hard time to explain that to people. How come is that possible? They were asking me.

It was almost 2-3 a.m. o'clock that day when I entered the Unit B, where I was going to reside for 5 months. I was introduced to the officer in service that night. The accompanying officer told her that I requested to take my shower before I go to bed, it was a sealed deal and I was allowed to take my shower. I got soap from the officer and then took my shower. I didn't have lotion because I had to leave everything in the consign till the day I get out. My skin was dry; anyway the most important was my shower which helped me to forget where I was and I slept.

In the morning of October 2nd 2008, I woke up at the metallic sound of the prison door. I just started sleeping! I realized then that I didn't sleep at all in 24 hours. I learnt that the sleep time or the curfew was at 11 p.m. and the waking time was at 5H20. There was what they call count time, one at 11 a.m., one at 4 p.m., one at 11 p.m. Oh Lord, I was in prison; I woke up with patchy mouth, I was like throwing. I looked at myself and couldn't believe that I slept in the bunk, on that hard thin mattress and wearing a sport suit, which was the only item of my wardrobe. Beside this there was that unlovely dark bleu uniform for regular normal people and orange for the bad, red for the worst. No style in detention center. To complete the costume, I had to put on a tiny pair of china snickers, the cheapest ever. I don't remember where I have seen that type of shoes. That was my reality from then, to the day God grace would release me. I was quiet pleased that the idea of asking a certain type of uniform color never crossed my mind, there were some women when given the blue uniform, they asked the red or orange because these are more shinny. Oh no, you must know what those color stand for. The orange and red were worst, they were for those who have been convicted and coming from prison. I forgot the toilet bowl, it was right there in front of my nose by the entrance of the cell. I shared the room with another female and anytime she could use the toilet and she was sitting there, I had to ignore what she was doing even though from my bed which was the one in the bottom nothing could be missed. I had to ignore the stinky smell too.

I got out of my bed, brush my teeth and stood at the door looking down at the sitting area. I noticed a line, there was no buffet in the Detention Center. I didn't know if I should line up to get my breakfast or just stood there and look at those women. I felt humiliated, diminish, worthless. I never line up for food in my life as a free woman unless I am helping myself at the buffet, things were different since I gave up all my freedom by being locked up. At that point, I couldn't think of how much price for my freedom. No there is no price for freedom, the Detention Center is not a place for happy hour. From inside it looks like a jungle within walls. Just as you enter the Unit B, you bump into the officer desk and in the opposite side you have an alignment of metal bench where detainees spent time talking, conspiring against each other and swearing. Behind the benches there are beds that are visible to everybody, they are extra bed where the unlucky client who didn't have a chance of getting a room will spend few days. Being assigned a bed outside was like being on the market. The place was usually packed and noisy; girls were talking and laughing so loud. Most were like, no you people you need to listen to me. We were all coming from different countries/Continent Asia, America, South America (Mexico, Guatemala, Honduras, Brazil), Europe, Africa, and Canada. To be franc that place was full of Mexicans, this was the first impression. Detainees also have different background, some have been there for crossing the border without visa, for being in US without legal documents, for DUI or drug crime and specially for having 3 strikes of crimes. So who will you hang with? It was difficult to get attached because everybody was stranger to everybody. I knew that the only way I would survive the Detention Center was to stay out of trouble and being courteous to all without preference and also show love to all those ladies who have been separated from their family, even though they looked crazy in some ways by being loud or dancing dirty dance, deep inside they were sad and all that was to mask the pain.

The first day I was filled with emptiness, I was missing everybody, my family, my friends, I was missing the pleasure of spending my evenings watching the debates, on CNN and MSNBC, watching David Gergen, Gloria Bolger, Donna Brazile, Larry King, Wolf, Martin, Anderson, Campbell, Bagala, John King etc . . . did I miss anyone? They were a part of my life, I spent my solitary evenings watching the show. I could decline an invitation because the best team was on TV. I liked the fight, I liked the talk, I liked everything; David could say something . . . who was going to catch the ball and say something? Watching my favorite people on TV, was like sitting in the arena watching a basketball game or a wrestling match. David Bagala the "sharpest, the shark", this is how I called him I was like don't touch him, he his sharp and will cut you, he will bit you, he was always ready with the bomb. After Sarah Palin nomination he was like "No this is crazy, Mac is crazy!" that was a blast! It was the media frenzy in action every night. No I didn't miss anything, I watched all the primary, all the fights. Oh no, I just started knowing Tim Russett, and he left us? He was gone too soon, I was shocked, why? In all that who was my choice? I always liked Hillary and Bill, Hillary has been my favorite for long time, but this time it was like a revelation. I picked Barrack from the start and I stuck with him. I was defending him, I discussed with some friends about my choice and they were very surprise to see my confidence. I told my friends that I would bet for my candidate, if I could do so but one of the best lesson I have ever learned in my life, "never bet". The only stupid bet I had bet in my life was almost 18 years ago, I lost 10 gr of Gold, I sure to never bet anymore.

I was standing on the line ready to get my food when I was approached by a short strong lady who asked me to go sit with her group at one of the round table in the east side of the sitting area. She introduced herself my name is "Marianne" from Romania and then I said oh, this is my mother name! I like this name. I empathized and walked with her at her table where I was introduced to the women sitting all around and her daughter Alex. Marianne, Alex and Mary were coming from Sacramento. They experienced a bizarre treatment during their transfer to Seattle, then to TACOMA Detention Center. They have been handcuffed during their air trip to Seattlle and said that it was so embarrassing that they had to keep the cuff even while going to the toilet. During their transfer one of the officer was drank and was stating profanity against foreigners, was laughing at them and even kicked a Mexican guy. Marianne and the girls told me the funny story of their first night, they were so tired that they didn't even notice the ladder on the side of the bunk's bed, they were like jumping to reach the upper bed when someone stopped them and told them that they needed to use the ladder on the side of the bed other wise they might fall. They said that it was very funny and they didn't get how they could have missed the ladder. I quickly found out that those women even locked and away from all luxury life we all had at home, they still laughing and joking. I like to laugh and joke, I was sold but decided to still vigilant, I just met those people and I wasn't sure of how we were going to handle the pressure and support each other in our new community and environment. We briefly shared our stories and started talking, till there was nothing to say, then we started talking about people. As a believer I know gossip is not good, but I was looking to know what about who and see how to make my move. I noticed quickly that Marianne had an aversion against Mexicans. I asked her why was she mad at Mexicans? She said that is because of Mexicans that things are getting bad in USA and also because of them US has created the immigration detention center. I said oh wait why do you think that because of Mexicans you are paying? Mexicans seem to have given less or no credit even though their contribution to America is great, this because of the illegal entering in USA. How long have you been here? I asked her. Marianne has been in US for 18 years and never thought to regularize her papers and she was having nerves to blame Mexicans? So you have been here for 18 years and never mind to do your papers and you think that you are right and the Mexican in the same situation is wrong? How can you think that you are better than the Mexican? This was not fair and I knew then that I was going to defend Mexicans or who ever will be attacked unfairly. I hate injustice and I was going to stand and tell people the truth or tell them that they should treat other with respect. As soon as I empathize with Marianne I started regretting the fact that I accepted to rejoin her table. I noticed that she was cursing and treated Mexicans as worthless. I was compressing, my steam engine was boiling and I just decided to ignore her all the rest of the day. I should stay out of trouble, I didn't have to forget that I was in Tacoma Detention Center, an Immigration facility.

There were days where all detainees were down the hill, full of pessimism and lack of confidence. There eyes were full of sadness and tears. The magic of Christmas has started outside and it was very hard to imagine being locked at this period of the year. The television was all about Christmas shopping. We have been missing the joy of Christmas for something that could have been solved on humanitarian basis. Many have been locked for so long time. It was almost 3 months since I have been in Detention Center, my friend Erika from Mexico have been there for 3 years, another girl from Africa for 2 years, another from Haiti for 2 years. Most of them were sad and were crying every day. Most of them have kids under the age of 10 left with a friend or a family member. They have been crying because of their kids. The immigration had picked some people from work while kids were in school and not knowing what about there parents. They also picked some at home or on the street during a traffic control. The most difficult for those detainees is that the way the immigration was handling the immigration matter was not giving them chance to put some order in their business, talk to someone from children school or someone from the community. Beside that they considered that the immigration system was unfair, they considered that being kept in a detention center for so long was making them look like common criminals who are locked up in a Federal prison. They all didn't think that the immigration crime should be sanctioned by such long detention time. I asked Erika, Rahel and Carmelita why their cases were taking so long ? They told me that a decision has been made a long time ago and they were appealing and fighting their cases.

I was far away of thinking that I will be in detention center fighting the devil winds. The week of 7 December 2008 I felt like a firefighter who was called to rescue. We have been cracking on jokes that day, we have been laughing; we had good time. Then Erika who was locked for 3 years, changed her expression and became sunddenly sad. She was saying that it suck, she was tired and depressed. She first burned the 2 pieces of bread she had that evening in the microwave, it seems like that was the only food she had. Most of us had to do special cooking because the 2/3 of the tray was thrown in the trash. Many times I heard girls saying that "even my dog eat better food than that" What did I say? No, it was everyday that I heard that comment. The food was never good and on my part the only food that had real taste was the cake. Everything was processed food, can food, or rotten corn bread etc . . . kid portion, served on the brown tray, this gave that food the aspect of dogs food. It could pass 2 weeks without seing a piece of chicken. I was joking and saying that the Tacoma Detention was the only place in America where you have to pray to have chicken at lunch. Yes everybody was like praying for the chicken. Unfortunately that was luxury. This time of the year is a time to share with your love ones than staying locked in 3 square feet room, with the toilet right on your nose, with under bed as cabinet, and beneath mattress as safe where you keep your everything. To be able to have a good taste of bread in the mouth, we used to put them in the microwave where they dry and eat them with jelly, peanut butter, what ever we had. But that week end on Saturday and Sunday, the food was nothing. If you just have that to eat, you starve all week end. Erika just burned her toast, as she was trying to reach to trash can to throw the burned toast I saw her crying, I never seen her so depressed. She was the sunshine, the one who was making everybody laugh, she was the strongest and the leader. Every morning, in the cold weather, with a team of believers they were out praying that we had God mercy. Why was she crying? The friends who were sitting at our table started talking to her, encouraging her to stay strong . . . she was really upset. She said that she felt like a dog in the cage, the food, the brown tray on which the food was served, everything make it look like dog food. Really Jenny I feel like a dog, she insisted. Unfortunately that was the sad reality of our life in Detention. I walked Erika to her room. As I was standing at the door step, I said to myself, that I needed to pull some magic from my spirit to deal with this crises, Erika was crying and showing me her room that she has called home for 3 years, she mentioned "this is all space I have got for 3 years, can you believe that?" She said to me, what could I say, my room was the same and was still the same since the time I got in the Detention Center. No there was one difference, Erika was there for 3 years and to that day I was there for two months, I was convinced that soon I was going out. Even with my belief and faith, I felt sometimes weak; then I saw myself breaking down, I was like no, do something. I couldn't stop it, I couldn't hide it neither. I told Erika that it was ok to cry, and frankly I avoided to tell her that things were going to be fine, I was ashame of the world of the unfair decisions that are making people suffer. No, you can not keep telling someone who has been locked for 3 years that things are going to be fine and since nothing has happened. She has been counting days, how many thanksgiving, how m**any** Christmas, how many New Years. You can tell someone it is ok after a week, a month, few months, but it become difficult to keep saying that after a year, 2 years, 3 years. No this is so wrong. During Christmas the detention center delivers bags of goodies, Erika has kept hers since the first Christmas without opening them. I asked her, why she was keeping that with a big chance of expiration, then they will be worthless. She said that she wanted just to keep them since she promised her children that they were going to open those bags together the day she would be out. You know what the magic Christmas bags have brought to many, while opening them in presence of your family with your kids. Truly Christmas time in Detention Center is so sad, I don't know the words to describe what I have seen in each face of those women.

I was myself down and I didn't know what to tell to the ladies. I called my pastor, Jean Bruno Nzeye to tell him what was going on and asked him to put everybody in prayer. My sole source of strength and wisdom is the Lord Jesus, the only who is full giving and merciful. I had to push that button for us to be heard by the most powerful. I was like if God is sitting, he will stand for us. He should remember all the good I have done for his people, all good Erika has done for many in the Detention Center. Indeed late November and early December the Holy Spirit put in my mind to start spreading the words to the women. Erika and I devoted ourselves to share the words of the Lord, we have been leading prayers and giving advises. I told those women that they needed seriously to commit their life to Jesus and start praying. Not everybody welcomed that idea. I started talking to Maria Salas about Jesus and the faith, she was loving and very beautiful girl who didn't appear sufficient. She was so humble and wanted to learn about the faith, in Hebrews 11:1 faith is the substance of things hoped for, the evidence of things not seen. The faith becomes present in each one of us as soon as we accept Jesus, this is the work of the Holy Spirit. Hebrews 10:38 says Now the just shall live by faith. These words are God's words which are the truth. Many of us find difficult this truth, at the same time they want God to control their life, they want to do things themselves by cheating, stealing or corruption . . . those are short cut that most of the time led to the lost. I told her to commit everything in God hands and believe that he is powerful and able. We make God happy when we come back to him as small as little children and let him take control. Jesus is the author and the finisher of our faith Hebrew 12:2. In is name every knee shall bow, in His name walls break, the impossible become possible, all power of the enemies bow. I had to call God grace upon her and to open her ears, indeed it was surprising to see a big number of people who don't care, neither believed in God and on the other hand it is sometimes amazing to see how God works. Many have been running all those years thinking that they own everything they become and everything they have. They are running a lot after the material and money and forget who made that possible. But God has been watching and is time will come sooner or later where ones will be looking for someone stronger than money, stronger than a good friend, stronger than a connection, stronger than idolism of a husband or of a kid; everything shall pass. Most of the women in the detention appear not knowing anything about God or have heard about him before. Many forget that we don't own anything, nor our life and no matter how good and bad it can be. We have been created to fulfill God's purpose. In Matthew 7

(24-27) KJV, Jesus states "therefore whosoever hear these sayings of mine, and doeth them, I will liken him unto a wise man, which built his house upon a rock; and the rain descended, and the floods came, and the winds blew, and beat upon that house; and it fell not: for it was founded upon a rock. And every one that hear these sayings of mine, and doeth them not, shall be likened unto a foolish man, which built his house upon the sand. And the rain descended, and the floods came, and the winds blew, and beat upon that house; and it fell: and great was the fall of it". Maria was a kind of ready to listen and learn, she was very passionate and was asking questions. It was challenging to preach the faith to someone who never practice before and never experience the faith. Maria was a kind of ready to open the door to Christ and listen to the word. Most of the time we have a very bad approach of the subject or of how to teach people. We force them and expect them to change immediately. They are indeed subject to change and this change is not coming overnight. While we look not at the things which are seen, but at the things which are not seen: for the things which are seen are temporal; but the things which are not seen are eternal. "2 Corinthians 4:18". We need to put our attention beyond what we see. We need to visualize the accomplishment of the impossible, because with Jesus everything is possible. The promises are true and real, and we need to stay focus and wait patiently to see them pass.

After 2 days of work with Maria, I noticed that women where coming one by one and before long seats around the table couldn't be enough anymore. They were standing behind the seats, they were curious and were asking questions. Since most of them were not speaking English I then asked Maria to do the translation in Spanish. I was very happy to share the truth I know, and happy to bless someone since I was blessed. Let be delighted in giving our time to teach other, to help others get out of darkness. Everybody was indeed delighted and very happy to finally have peace of mind. Some asked for prayers, and I told them that everything will be given to you according to your faith and . . . LOVE. Many neglect the love part of this scripture; someone can come and ask for a prayer and think that "faith only is enough", its not possible to have a heart full of strife and anger and believe that this is ok, to please God in this way. Jesus is love, and this love is in my heart, I need to be free of strife if I want work to be manifest in my life. Don't forget "Faith and love" work together, you may have a faith of 40 years but without love, your faith is vain. Well I was telling the women that Faith and Love work together, what ever we get after we have asked and or sometimes we get things that we didn't even ask, is by God grace. But it is so important and serious we consider the purity of our spirit and heart while asking God favor. I saw many fighting for nothing against each other, many criticizing, cursing, insulting. I told them that, no this is not going to bring you any favor. 1 Corinthians 13 NIV says "and now these three remain: faith, hope and love. But the greatest for these is love. I was in the middle of the teaching when I saw Erika coming, she never came to the gathering before and I never forced her to do so. I assumed that since she was with one group early in the morning for prayers, maybe that was just enough for her. She was sitting listening and then as I finished the meeting and was walking to my bunk she followed me and said that she wanted to talk to me. I was standing at the door listening to her, I was shocked because she was telling me that I was too soft with the women and I should be hard on them and show them that they have to take the words as it is or nothing were going to happen. She mentioned that some were still watching television and gossiping, that I was petting them and they needed to change. Oh! Erika was getting jealous, in a matter of second I tried to insure her that I was not taking her spot, I was just sharing what the Holly Spirit has put in my mind for God's people. Beside this I don't think that watching TV was a sin, and I didn't see how I could address this subject without being judgmental. People were concern about what we call sins, and one of the girl Melinda, said that according to most of the preaching, everything people do is a sin, and it confused her; people think that religions is just a way of limiting people freedom, it is only focusing on sins(?). This is the consequence of the preaching that is condemning before teaching, condemning before showing love, before showing understanding and compassion; it takes time to change. Those teachings have made people run away from the truth. God's will is liberty and people should be confident to live there life in Jesus and not live in fear. God love has been given to us by grace. 2 Corinthians 3:17 says "now the lord is that spirit: and where the spirit of the Lord is there is liberty", Jesus came to set at liberty those are bruised, he came to set the captives free. God is doing so much to show us how much he loves us, in return we will show our love to him by keeping his commandments which free us from condemnation. Philippians 1:6 says "I am sure that God who began the good work within you will keep right on helping you grow in his grace until his task within you is finally finished on that day when Jesus Christ returns. Erika was more worry to change people than letting the Holly Spirit do his work, which start inside each one of us. The Holly spirit work will grow little by little like a dot of light that is shining from miles deep inside you and surface as a bright light outside wiping the darkness. Your spiritual ground and physical ground will surrender little by little. By listening and reading the words, the spirit will guide you in making good choice and some stuff you might have enjoyed doing, saying, looking at will be just worthless. The person we have become has been formed during a long process and many years, everything we have become is a second nature which has its roots deep inside us. None of us can by its force change this nature if God didn't intervene. Who can tell about what is in the heart, someone has said that the heart is a suitcase full of clothes. You may put all the clothes out without noticing what the bottom of the case is made of. I wasn't competing with Erika, I told her I was just doing what the Spirit was putting into my mind.

What I noticed later is that we were having answers to our prayers, and every time I was happy and praising the Lord, even though it was obvious that I was praising Jesus, Erika could pass by and said. All that has been done for the glory of Jesus not for the glory of one person. Of course it was for the Lord and it will always be. I was sad and was afraid that this fight would weaken the work I was doing or would discourage me. I remember that we have been praying for a Mexican woman who came to see her son who was laying down in the hospital while waiting for a kidney transplant. I am sure that God answered that prayer, Erika started to give testimony, and then she stopped and spoke in Spanish promising she will share the news with me later, she refused to translate and up till today she never confirm what I apparently knew. I knew that it was that case we prayed for, I knew that this young man got healed. And the day his mother left the detention center, she never say good bye. Anyway, I did everything for the glory of the Lord. Erika is my friend and sometimes we just need to love unconditionally to make it work and be above all devil works. Jealousy, competition among children of the Lord doesn't do any good to the church or to any group that has been formed for God glory. We don't need to compete and praise human being. The bible said that the field is big and need workers, there are multi ministries defined by the Holy Spirit gifts and each one of us should be able to find from deep inside what his calling is and serve accordingly. I wish Erika had her eyes at that time fixed on the Lord than on me or on what I was doing. I didn't want to be distracted, but I know she was distracted. I was very sad for her and I tried my best to help her feel confident, I helped her with teaching and I wonder if she was teachable. In 2 Chronicles 26 the word is talking about "developing a teachable spirit before God". Erika was trying to contradict some stuff I was telling her, and I showed her that in God business we are basing ourselves on the truth, which is the word. I was reading the word to help her understand and then she was like "ah you are right", no I wasn't right, the word was is right and it is the truth. With love and patience I made her understand what I was doing.

I had noticed a girl who was very loud most of the time, and seemed at the same time when of the sad person ever. Such contrast, the same person could be loud and high and show a very broken spirit. The girl was Cecile, a Phillipino girl from Alaska, who needed help. Indeed God put into my mind to pray for her. Before I was deeply involved in God business, it was like am I crazy? Why do I think that I can go and talk to this girl? How is she going to react? And so on . . ., but since I have learned the work of Holly Spirit I don't fear the failure, I don't fear the rejection. And what is interesting is that even though the first time the answer could be negative, the Holly Spirit would be doing is work by pushing you to try again and again and at the same time he would be working on the other person. You can guess that it was not easy with Cecile, I tried to talk to her the first time the Holly Spirit asked me to pray for her, but she was like "I will see, I have something to do, I will see you later" I tried to go slowly and took time to learn what was her problem. I quickly understood that she felt her mother didn't love her very much, she has put her down all her life, telling her "you are capable of nothing, you are nothing, you will be never anything". I was choked and truly there a big number of girls who have lost the self esteem because of the abuse situation they have been since childhood with a no loving father or mother. Children are given to us by God grace as a gift, and they are God's children. Who ever has a child is holding him/her for God, therefore we have an obligation to love them and cherish them. We have an obligation of taking care of them, of teaching them and blessings them. Blessings kid is so important and I wonder why many are not taking that seriously. In Genesis 27 Isaac has blessed Jacob the youngest with the first born blessings instead of blessing Esau, I wish, someone would understand what happened when Esau learned that his youngest brother, was blessed with what could have been his blessings. The bible says in Genesis 27 (34-38), "and when Esau heard the words of his father, he cried with a great and exceeding bitter cry, and said unto his father, bless me, even me also, o my father . . . And Esau said unto his father, hast thou but one blessing, my father? Bless me, even me also, o my father, and Esau lifted up his voice and wept. How important it is that we bless our children, the blessings words as any word has a power of doing good when the word is a blessing word or has the power to destroy when it is cursing. I was sad for Cecile, I talked to her and encourage her to ignore whatever her mum has said to her. I told her God has made her beautiful and intelligent. I told her to believe in God and soon or later if she believes she will see how happy she was going to be. After she has run from me for many days, I praid for her and give her coached her with life lessons. She was convinced that she was nothing and she was going to be deported. She was spending her time crying or yelling of rage. I was praying for her on my own or with friends, then I saw that she was scratching, her skin was eachy and was bleeding. I asked Jesus to heal Cecile, and I remind him that I asked the healing gift and I wanted to show me that this was possible through Cecile. After a month, Cecile was free of skin desease, she was free and left the detention center.

Rachel from Alaska, the girl from from London and Mary a Fidji girl who use to live in California were leaving the Detention Center. The magic was at our table, people looking at us like a miracle happened among us. We were making noise and praising the Lord for those releases. We were going to miss the good time, we have been joking and laughing. I did my best to stay friendly with everyone and specially welcomed everyone who wanted to sit at our table, since I had something to teach; but one thing I was sure of is that most of them were afraid of me, afraid of my acknowledge, they were surprised that I knew so much and only few didn't like me for that. I was talking to an officer and I told her that I have a Bachelor Degree in Law, Maria took that as an offense. Later on she said, you have a Bachelor Degree, why are you here? I told Maria that it was not my fault that I know so much, unfortunately for her I went to school, I was blessed and what I have learned stay with me, live with me and die with me. It was like if she was asking the sun to not show up, that is impossible. Such a joy and relief to learn that those girls were going home. Richel the girl from Phillipino who lived in Alaska was such a nice sweet girl. She was a true blessing for who ever was around her. She was sharing phone card, helping everyone in need. I talked to Richel and advised her during her staying in detention center. Since she was arrested on possession of drug, I thought that I should helped her with wise talk that could help her not to go back to drug business. Dr. Schuller reading inspired me a lot, and I shared some with Richel. According to Dr. Schuller "Iron pilloned people don't fall apart when life falls in because they have instinctive capacity to weigh the alternatives and see their options. Most of time people who are faced with problems say that they have only one choice. That's not true, in every situation you face, you will always have at least four alternatives: You can quit, you can back down and retreat, you can pause and wait or you can fight to hold your ground and advance, however slowly, toward your goal." This was so true, Richel was arrested because of bad choice and was about to lose her green card; luckily she was going home to Alaska. I talked to her, I gave her advises like a big sister to a little sister. I truly liked her, she always listen, she was polite and was so humble. She looked like the best young lady ever. All her family came from Alaska to attend her hearing. That is love and so awesome. I was concern that she would not be able to hug her son or any other member of her family at the court. Indeed she was not allowed to do so. Her son was crying, her mom was crying and couldn't give her testimony. Anyway it was over, she won her case. She left very happy and looked like a new person. She mentioned that she has learned the lesson and she thanked me for helping, for coaching her with life's lessons. We have been very happy to see Richel leaving.

Every morning was a new start and new story. I specially enjoyed morning time from Monday to Friday, during this period there was life in the Detention Center. Weekdays were actives because of movement due to the court, you have decision made, you see people leaving, people coming in. No, they just leave during the week and come in every day, every morning, every evening, every night. When you check in, you are kept in a cold freezing waiting cell for up to 8 hours before being assigned to a room. This is why some check in at 2 a.m., 4 a.m.

In the morning of December 12th 08, I didn't get out for breakfast. I slept late and I staid in my bed. Since Erika didn't see me outside, she came to check on me and I told her that I was staying in my bed and relax. After I got out, I learned that the Russian/Romania team had left. Yes! That was so good, finally peace at the end . . . The Russian team was the team formed by Marianne and her daughter, they are Romania but originally from Russia. The daughter who was 18 at that time, seems to be wise and smart. And she was the opposite of her mom, it was like day and night. Marianne was crazy and versatile. You never know what to expect from her. Just one time, just one time she tried to be funny. I told her that she had to treat her daughter very well, she has a very special daughter. She looked at me and say what? She is special? I said yes, she is precious. She said it's ok that you said she is precious and nice, but don't ever say she is special. I had hard time to understand what she was trying to say, coming from French culture "special" means "particular, unique, exceptional, precious" I wanted to understand, then I asked her to explain. Why I shouldn't said that Alexandra is special; she told me that many years ago Alexandra was preparing herself to go to one of well known and best school in California, she was ready with everything except her mom had to answer to one particular question asked by telephone : she was at home when the school called her and asked her if her daughter was "special", she was still on the phone and she yelled at her daughter "Alex, Alex I am on the phone with your new school, they are asking if you are special, tell me aren't you special?" Yes mom I am, she then told the guy on the phone. Yes my daughter is special (?) She told me that Alex never got a chance to go to that school because in English being "special" means "medical/physical condition". She didn't know at that time and I didn't know neither, we never learn enough. Nevertheless Marianne was one of the weakest person I have ever met, unhappy, complaining, cursing Mexicans, insulting people because somewhere she was like above all and thinking that she deserved the best. Marianne spirit was destructive, she was sniching. She was so bad, not loving people at all, to the point that the women called her "snake" Oh, when someone call you "snake" it's very bad. You need to check yourself. The day before they left during lunch time, we have been lining up when Richel who was about to leave the center, said "I am going to miss everybody", Marianne jumped into that and said "oh no, no I am not going to miss anyone". I just thought that this was really devil and wicked, she had a stone in place of bloody heart. I couldn't believe what I just heard! That was the type of people who never want to die by themselves and would like that everybody die with them, everybody had to drown with them. For no money She would be happy and specially happy to see someone happy. Am I talking about the same person who upon my arrival in the Detention Center run to me, and welcomed me? As soon as she saw me she came to me trying to act nice and then next thing I knew I was sitting in the east side of Unit B at the big round table called "international table"?. For Marianne, everybody should be miserable since she was unhappy; she was fighting people for TV, clothing because she allowed herself to steal changing sweater while folding laundry (uniform, sweater, sweater pant). She was fighting Mexican and saying that they are the one who created the immigration tension. She was like really all her unhappiness was created by Mexicans. I fought with Marianne over Mexicans comments. I remember the day where she was sitting and having attitude when she asked so stupidly "tell me why Mexican government doesn't keep is people and why are they so pour?" I said "what?" She repeated what she just said. I was very happy, because I had arguments, I could defend an intellectual point of view and shut Marianne down. I first of all asked why she came to USA? She avoided my question, I then started teaching her a lesson that I knew she would never forget: I told her that if those people had everything, they wouldn't have come to US, and that they are not poor; they are hard working people it's why they are here. Besides this most of the government are trying to manage their people and everybody is trying to look for a better life where ever it's possible. Actually most of the world population is in survival mode and it's a complex political/economic agenda, then you can not just talk like that to people. Also somewhere I told her: you know, you might have come from Europe, Romania, or wherever I still remember how my country Congo helped Romania during Mobutu era in seventies, Mobutu had factories in your country which employed your people. For sure she didn't know that part of history, she consciously forgot that her own country still poor. Marianne was shocked, I shut her down; when she left our table, I wasn't sure that she was going to talk to me again, I didn't care! She was the last of my worries. Later on Marianne tried to go back to her mean nature, I was still standing and fighting back; she had to cop with that and live with Mexicans. Common, she was immigrant like everybody, why was she thinking that she was entitled to better consideration than others. She was dam racist, I heard that she even said some stuff against black people. One evening Erika was singing in Spanish in the shower, she was even fasting. When Marianne listened to Erika singing, she yield toward her "can you sing in English?" Erika looked at her without any interest of pursuing any kind of discussion or fight, I could see Erika's hazelnut killer eyes looking at Marianne. Luckily she didn't say anything and she ignored her. Marianne should blame herself for what was happening to her. She had people who were willing to help her with advice concerning her immigration case but she was like, no we want to go back to Romania. The next day she was like no, we want to stay. Really what did she want? Nobody could understand what was going through her mind, she was in fight with the officer in charge of her case, pushing for her travel documents, then when the documents were ready, she was like, oh no I don't want them anymore. She spoke to another lady and asked her if she could help by asking her lawyer to intervene and stop the removal process. She was very crazy, she pushed for that, she didn't want to listen to those who were advising her. She was most of the time like "no I know what to do, Mrs. Right". She was like knowing it all . . . most of the time when people pretend knowing everything, really they are just pretending and don't know everything. I wish I never meet this woman, she was drama queen . . . The Romania departure in the morning of December 12th 08 was indeed the first big news of the day.

As I was going to sit at the round table, international table, I saw a young lady sitting on one of the outside bed; she was beautiful and it was easy to read the sadness on her face. She has been crying, I approached her,

I said hi and I asked her what brought her in the Detention Center. She told me that she was a newlywed, she got married the previous weekend! Her wedding took place later than expected because of her mother in law death, she had a lot going on in her life and who cares, she was brought in Detention Center. Her mother in law must have been a loving person because when she mentioned her, she broke in tears, that was painful to see, she was from Australia her name is Cassi. As soon as she got married she filed her papers and according to her, her husband had paid a substantial amount to the immigration for her papers. Nevertheless she was caught somewhere at the border where she has been visited with the family. I shared my own story with her and told her that she needed to stay strong and stop crying. She told me that when she checked in at 9 p.m. and was assigned to a room around 2 a.m. At the border she was kept for 8 h. She had a glass of water as the only meal in 24h. She was very upset and couldn't understand what was happening. Erika helped her with phone cards, she called her husband who later fought hard to get a very good lawyer who could help her get out. She didn't touch her lunch, she refused to eat. After lunch I went to my room and few minutes later, Erika came to tell me that the Australian girl was leaving. I was very happy for her, She was happy and wanted to see me before she left. I came down in to the sitting area to say good by. After she left, I then learned that her husband was one of the big guy in sport environment. He has got a powerful lawyer, who has brought media with her. As far as I can remember the Immigration doesn't like media involvement and scandals. Having cameras in front of the Immigration facility wasn't good news. We were very excited and happy to see that some good case and high profile could help the rest. By getting out the message, we had a chance of seeing some changes. Money talks, said someone; another girl standing by said "this means that since I don't have money I am going to be locked up here for good? I turn myself and touched her and said to her "you know, your case can be released by the most powerful, the one who is above all," she smiled at me as to say your are right. The cameras/the journalists at the immigration facility can be time to time a very good idea. There are many things, many stories that need to be told; it was hard for me to think that one day stay in the Detention Center could cost $100. The bunk cost even more than a hotel room at a Day Inns Hotel where you have 2 beds, a TV, a fridge, telephone, bathroom, iron . . . this is crazy, anyway None of us believed in that. The food was catastrophe, very cheap. I said to myself even if who could eve served with a MC Do meal, this amount would never be so high.

I know that money is not everything, but it is necessary. I am not obsessed by money and will not let it control my life, but what many don't understand is that we have been excited all day by Cassi's story and have been talking about that all day long. In the evening after Cassi's has left, we have been sitting at the round table for dinner when excited I tried to recall Cassi's story's and I commented by saying "you know, she is a millionaire". I don't remember something else that I have said that could be bad, hurtful or offending to any one at our table, but my good friend Erica got offended and said: you know what, I don't care about millions, what I care about the most is my Lord Jesus. I received that like a slap into my face, I started defending myself by telling her that God comes 1st in my life, but we still live in the world where we need money, and if someone like Cassi has money, this means that she has been blessed. Besides this I consider myself God's heir, I should then inherit everything from him. If God is rich, I should be rich too. I know that money is not everything and I am not obsessed by it. But what people should know is that we have money in us, we all have a gold mine inside us. We just need to allow the potentiality that is within to glow, to show. God made us like that and we should know it, we need to find the way to dig a little bit inside us to get that gold out and be rich spiritually, materially and in everything area of our life. You can be rich in joy, in giving, in sharing, in helping, in blessing. Dr. Schuller Robert in his book "living positively one day at a time" talked about the treasure within each one of us and said : "God carefully, quietly hides his most precious gifts so that may become joyous by discovering them. It is an universal truth that the greatest most valuable treasures are hidden from clear view. The pearl is hidden within the oyster beneath the deep waters of the ocean. The diamond is buried deep within the earth and the gold nuggets are concealed within the sides of mountains. Also the greatest of God's treasures lie neither beneath the sea, within the earth or in distant heavens. God's greatest treasure lies within you and me, the resource of human creativity and potential! Within you are gems of incredible value pearls of great price." Pastor Copeland in his book "Faith to Faith", is asking us to strike it rich. According to the bible Galatians 3:29 says "and if ye be Christ's, then are ye Abrham's seed and heirs according to the promise". Pastor Copeland says that "one of the problems that hung around him for years was poverty. But he remember the day he decided he wasn't going to be poor anymore. He was reading in the word where it says that the blessing of Abraham has come upon the Gentiles by Jesus Christ (Gal. 3:14). Then he got down to the twenty-ninth verse where it says, "IF YE BE CHRIST'S THEN ARE YE ABRAHAM'S SEED,

AND HEIRS ACCORDING TO THE PROMISE". Also Deuteronomy 28 says "blessed in the city, blessed in the country, blessed going out, blessed coming in. Blessed in your barns, blessed in your fields, blessed in all the works of your hands".

I was sad, very sad to see that my friend Erika couldn't even accept the fact that we are different, and we should accept everyone as he is. Anyway, a moment later we tried to make peace and move on . . . Even though I wanted really to close Cassi's chapter, later in that evening my friend show me a big number of phone card she had received from Cassi, isn't money good?

The major attraction of the detention Center was the coming in and going out of detainees. They were coming from everywhere, they were not only Mexicans.

I still remember Faiz, the girl from London who came to the Detention Center on December 15th 2008; she was so young and naïve, she came to see her husband and got locked up because the last time she came to US she overstayed then she lost her visa weaver. She was trying to come to visit her husband, unfortunately the past mistake came to catch her. She got caught at the airport and brought in Detention Center. She was crying as everybody on the first day in Detention. I then invited her to our table, we shared our mutual stories and then I found out that she traveled with a good friend of 2 years who came along to meet a guy she was involved in virtual romantic relation. Since Faiz was locked up, her friend was picked up by her husband and headed home with him till the mysterious man come to pick her up. I know personally what those youngsters are made of or are capable of, because at that age many are looking for adventure, they are instabile in love, and not always looking for the right guy. Most of them play around or act like everything is allowed, no trespassing zone can work for those youngsters, the limit is the sky for them. Then I quickly realized how young and naïve Faiz was. I asked her if her friend where going to stay with her husband. She said yes and somewhere she mentioned that since the strange girl was her friend, there was nothing wrong with her staying at Faiz place. Indeed in general the youngster seem to appear kind and nice till you face the threat and fill betrayed by the one you trusted and the one you gave your soul to. Since Faiz was confident, I didn't pursue the talk. But I a kind of took risk by telling Litia, another girl from Alaska who was sharing the table, that I wasn't sure that Faiz and her friend would still friend at the time Faiz will get out of detention center. We just laughed about and that was it. Nevertheless, not longer that 48 h later I overheard Faiz who was very loud, she was screaming on the phone, she was upset, nervous, and cursing.

There was trouble in paradise, things changed faster than I predicted. The drama started when she called her husband and couldn't get in touch with him, she tried many times and she was trying to find out where was he at? Hey, she was the boss and was so right . . . After she calmed down I asked her how her husband was doing. She said that he was fine, but something bothered her. Her husband just told her that he doubt that her girl friend is a good friend. She was talking more about her wasted vacation and going out than about her friend who was locked up. The girl friend wasn't wasting her time, she put herself to work pretty earlier than her good friend could imagine. Her husband also mentioned that she was deploying her seductions and sex appeal tricks with A list charm. She was flirting with him . . . then he asked her why did she think that this girl was her good friend and also why did she brought her? The girl friend was trying hard to catch Faiz's husband attention. She was dressing hot, she asked Faiz's husband if she could cook for him, but he declined. That guy was clever, sometimes the way to the heart can be through the stomach. Faiz was mad and I told her to remember that her friend was the girl she described few hours earlier as a good friend of her and that the 1st day she spoke about her, I have told Litia that they are not going to be friend the time she will get out of Detention Center. She asked me why I said so and I told her that I knew young people, and most of them don't care about hurting other feelings, neither about AIDS or putting their life in jeopardy for so little, for 15 minutes of sex. Most of them aren't appreciative of life, they do not treasure life and do not give life its value. Besides that many would like to sleep with your husband or your wife, and it seems so easy to have false impression on the unknown life of other people and envy for the forbidden? But the reality most of the time turns to nightmare. An old African adage says: you don't know how much someone roof is leaking till you go inside. Following Faiz phone conversation with her husband, she was expecting his visit, of course with the girl friend. They came to visit the next day, and after saying hello to FAIZ, the girl friend was so embarrassed that she went to sit in the car during the 45 minutes visit time. It was over, Faiz knew that then she couldn't keep trusting the girlfriend; after 5 days in detention she went back to London.

Tacoma Detention Center seems to be the center of the world sometimes, all the world was there: Canadian, Mexicans, Africans, Europeans, Asians . . . There was always a surprise while waking up in the morning there was a surprise of meeting new faces. In the morning of December 16th 2008 at 5H30 I just helped myself with the breakfast tray, not very much. I was interested in biscuits and milk which I would take later, then I saw Erika coming toward me, she had news for me, there was a sister from Africa on the other side of the sitting area who just booked in and she was in tears. Erika suggested that we should go and talk to her and eventually invite her at our table. I then went to talk to that lady and the only think I remember is that she was from Nigeria. Definitely one from Africa, a sister close to home I said. Erika and I introduced ourselves and talked to this lady whom I don't know her name, I didn't even asked the name. I asked her to stop crying, she was pregnant and that wasn't good for her to keep crying. We shared our story and I insured her that we have good people in the Detention Center who had issues with Immigration and it was just matter of time. She kept crying and telling me she had hard to understand what was going on. She had her visa from the American Embassy in Nigeria and that she didn't do anything wrong. I told her to keep quiet and that if really there is nothing wrong with her visa, she was going to get out anytime soon. No, brother there was something fishy, for the first visit she got 2 years visa man? It was her first visit, at this point I couldn't buy that story anymore. I was sure that this sister was going back to where she was coming. Anyway the immigration told her that she couldn't stay because she had an advanced pregnancy and it looks like she came to USA to give birth. Erika helped her to make some phones calls that didn't go through, she kept defending herself and at one point I told her that I know the American Embassy very well and there was no way that a visitor visa could exceed 6 months. Also to have more than a year or 2 years visa, you must be professional, have a contract or be in school. That was the truth, she had a fake true visa. I was sorry for her because she had to fly back by the next flight and that was a lot of money.

The Detention Center is full of diversities with diverse personality. I was interested in all, I had something to say, something to teach, I always captured something in someone etc . . .

There were some lesbian girls who spices life in detention center, they were flirting, kissing and as soon as they have been watched, people were talking and the officer was cursing. Do I have something interesting about this? Sure, frankly I didn't like my look; the day I enter the detention center I had extension, and I was wearing hearing, my jewelry, I was lady like. But after 3 months in Detention, I had to take off my extension, without make up, oh my I looked like a boy without hearings, my short hair wasn't helping. I hated myself, I see Lucy the lesbian girl coming to check on me when I was playing basket, and I left the court without saying anything.

Even those people who were close to me, Oh Emma, again Emma she looked at my hands and she said, Jenny you have big hands you should have been playing basket ball. I never notice before that I had big hands, I feel blessed that God created me whole, and healthy. Why do I have to check all parts of my body and see what is good what is not good? What surgery would change big hands to small hands? Really I like this part of me that make me strong even though sometimes, nothing in this way bothered me, those comments sound stupid to me and it is always easy for me to shut my ears. Another day Erika came so close to me, she was looking at me and then she said, oh you have a mustache (?) I said Erika stop that, she said yes look it is here, she pulled one of my hair above my superior lip, since then I shave to not get embarrassed again. Eh I felt a little, what it called they were putting me down. People can be though on you sometimes, but keep still stand. I can easily understand when someone is not a strong person and is going through all this, I understand how people lose their self esteem or why people do things to please other even though they are not happy with it, and even though they don't have the power to change it. I was not going to shrink my hands to be beautiful to the eyes of handful people. Then the meaning of "beauty" is relative while considering the external body aspect. Everybody is beautiful as human being, I always think that beauty is from inside, the joyful spirit inside you that makes your light shine outside that is what I call "beauty".

Around the December 15th I met Duce, she is from Mexico and when she checked in the Detention Center, she was assigned to my room as my roommate. She seems so intelligent, very worried and troubled. I offered to pray for her, we prayed the first day and then she told me that she didn't have anything to hide, she was coming from prison where she spent 4 years on drug charge. She was regretting that and will never go back to that business again. She was the only child of her mum who never got married with her father because she found out that the guy was living high risky life. He was in all bad illegal business in Mexico. Her mum had a deal with that guy who asked her to promise never contact him, never look for him. He was the one who was going to contact her and provide for her and the baby. There was a fight between her mum and the guy, she asked him to get out of her life. Her mum gave birth to her and raised her with the love and help of her grand parents. Her family was hardworking family and she really appreciated their hard work and all they have done for her. At early age Duce had a son who is actually eleven. Indeed sometimes people get bored of their quiet and regular life and want it little spicy and high. Also the envy and the dream of being big to soon to fast, make people at any age to decide for very bad choices. Duce told me that before she got into prison, coming to USA was every youngster dream. It was see America then die. She was contacted by a group of people, who considered themselves business men, who came with a huge business proposal. The proposition was for her to help them smuggle drug into America. They promise that nothing was going to happen to her. The first trip they paid her $ 5000.00, somewhere she manage to buy a house. She hide the drug into her car and crossed the American border with it. The 1st time, first try, she succeeded. She had to deliver the drug to her boss's cousin in a shop at the border. The boss insured Duce that everything was going to be fine, so easy say . . . she believed that and she enter the shop to talk to the receiver of the pack. Once outside where she went to get the pack at her car, the fish net was right on her head, she was surrounded by the police. She was lost, she said that she felt like the ground was crumbling under her feet. She was shaking, before even she picked her bag or anything in the car, the next thing she knows it that the police told her she was under arrest and that she had the right to remain silent and talk in presence of her lawyer. She was crying, nothing tears can help in this condition. It was too late, the damage was done. She was then sentenced to 4 years in prison. She missed her son, her mom, her grand parents, life, the freedom . . . That was a very sad story. I talked to her and asked her if she learned the lesson, she told me "yes and she thinks that was stupid, she doesn't know what was she thinking and that was the biggest mistake of her life". I told her that drug wasn't the only way she could make money. She then told me that she wish she had the power to discourage all young people who really believe in that stupid and delusional business. I told her that even with little work done seriously with commitment you can still make it. Do not just rush blind into life this way. Also all wasted time, that you will never get back? I believe that there is always a way to make a wise choice. Duce told me she regretted so much that she didn't allowed herself a minute pause to think wisely, money seems to be everything at that time. She added that what is really bad is that nobody is telling you the truth, somewhere it comes out like the best business in the world that is making everybody rich, and then it is as if you have caught the moon. I am sure that naivety and ignorance have brought many to that lost. Duce added that what is pathetic in this business is that you think doing it for a short period of time, then it becomes tasty, you want more and more . . . then you end up trapped in shopping addiction buying stuff like shoes, everyday more and more shoes. I saw tears on her eyes and then she asked: tell me what is it really for? What frankly could I say? I looked at her and asked her to promise to never go back to that business, she has to think that she might not be lucky the next time to get away with 4 years jail sentence and that might shut her life for good. She looked at me and then said you know what? It's not worth it . . . Indeed many never wonder, the objective is money and more money. Duce and I prayed a lot that night and I was like ok, she seems troubled, maybe she will find some good sleep and peace of mind. Oh no, the next day she told me that she was very anxious, somewhere she was wondering if she was ever going to make it out of the Tacoma Detention Center. She said that she was afraid she could die before she had a chance to get out. It was hard for me to understand what was going through her mind. I then told her: but Duce you are here for 2 or 4 days at least then you will be gone for Mexico, what is troubling you so much? She told me that she didn't think that she had to spend any single day in another detention facility after 4 years in prison. She was thinking that her getting out of jail was synonym of freedom, she was seeing herself going home the same day. She said that she saw 2 girls dying in the prison where she was, she was so scared. I told her that she had to be happy because she was on her way home. She told me that she didn't think that she had to spend another night locked up, she was supposed to go to Mexico the next day she was released from the Federal jail. I was burned by a poignant question since the first time she told me her story but I was looking for the good moment to ask and I caught an occasion and I asked her: Duce, tell me something, you took someone money to do drug and you lost it, what are you going to explain to him? Are you going to have contact with him? Do you know that you can get killed? She was shaking and looked like lost, but anyway she found the strength to tell me that she wasn't going to contact her former mafia boss. Are you sure that this is going to be enough? I asked her. They know where your family live right? I asked her again. Yes she answered, I was powerless but somewhere it came to my mind that I had to say a protection prayer for her. We said a prayer and she slept hoping that she is going to leave anytime soon. The 3rd day, she was still there and was like crying. In the evening of the 3rd day, she was told that her name was on the list, departure time that night. She ran toward me and gave me a big hug. She was very happy, I was also happy for her. In the middle of the night that day while sleeping I heard the cell door opening and the officer calling Duce, it was around 2h00 in the morning. She was excited and just wanted to get out. I hug her and I wished her good luck, I hope that she made it and she has good life in Mexico, many have been killed during 2008. I was a little bit sad for her, because of the uncertainty of the life she was going back to, but I was happy on the other hand that she opened herself to me and I was glad that I gave her all advises I had. She was talking like a very nice person who deserved a good life.

I was in acquaintance with many girls, I interact easily and I never regret that even though many times not all the people I meet are good people. I transcend and life goes on, we are not called to be alike, and even different we can still work together. Each one of us has something to bring to the table, t hat is the world.

Litia packed by giving away some food she bought from the commissary. For 2 weeks now, since I couldn't buy food because I didn't have money in my account, I was like starving most of the time. For lunch I had one little ball bread and a spoon of spinach. I was already thinking that I was going to starve that evening as the day before because most of the time lunch was poor, there was strong probability of having the same food in the evening. Erika brought bottles full of spices and among them was one pack of noodles. I don't know how it landed into my hand, no Litia gave that to me . . . I was like why did I get that? Why me? Do you know what, that was an answer to my prayer. I needed some extra food in the evening. Some nights I slept with an empty stomach, so were many of us. This noodles pack was like a Christmas gift. When time came for Litia to say good bye, I cried. Many said good bye to her, I remember the Korean lady who said good bye and cried, another one came and did the same, Erika also came to say good bye. The separation was always emotional. For the short period of time we spent together, we tried to bound and sustain each other in prayers and advices. We shared food, our fear and misery then life goes on. When I said good bye to Litia I understood that thinks were not going to be the same for me inside the Detention Center, she was like the only person real, most of them were fake. Since most of the girls from the international table left, Litia was the only one I hang out with. Erica and another lady from Salvador "Delmis" seem to be so busy in their room preparing Christmas gifts for their friends and family. It was amazing what Erika was capable of creating from scratch, she uses paper to do art craft, she uses soap, everything she could find. Such creativity, she was very gifted and she was like not recognizing it, it was amazing how she could make a bible from the soap, how she could make a tiger or a dog with soap paste . . . that was the good way of spending time in detention center instead of sitting at a table talking and when good talk dried up, you start cursing or criticizing people. I felt so lonely and empty when Litia left, I was sitting at my table almost by myself, looking around and few girls joked with me. I said to myself that I was going to be fine, I was going to get out of the Detention Center. Anyway the next day was a new day.

On December 19th 2008, I have been praying for Leticia, for her sick mum and sister, some people have a very though life. Comparing to what we some times complain about, you ask yourself how this person is handling things like the lost of all members of the family, like everybody has cancer in the family. What makes those people going, what makes them strong? Leticia mum and sister had cancer, she was on deportation and she wishes to pay anything to stay and take care of them. Unfortunately that Friday 19th of December, the decision was made against her and nobody could reverse it. I was sitting as every evening after diner chatting with girls before I go back to my room, when the officer started calling names of deported. This time Leticia was on that list, and it was the 3rd time she has been called. They have called her 2 times before and she had to be brought out of the unit at 2 a.m. for the check out, but every time she was processing the check out formalities, she was told that it was a mistake and then she was brought back to the unit. I really wish for her that this 3rd time was the good one. I have been telling Leticia that it was good to cry since she was crying, this will help to release the pain and the stress. I told her that she has to know that besides our plan, there is God plan which is the best and I emphasize that most of the time it's hard to quit because of our attachment to our life and everything material. I told her that the best act of faith was to leave everything to God. I told her that Abraham had faith that God raises from death to life, it's why he didn't hesitate to sacrifice ISAAC. This is very hard to understand without faith or the knowledge of God existence. We then prayed and I declared that we were not defeated, even though she was going, there was a victory at the end and God's ways are different from our ways and they are the best. I gave her my final advices and somewhere I see that she was going to fight to come back. Here is where I had problem with most of my friends, most of them were telling me that they were coming back without or with paper. I was strongly against to see my friends risking their life by trying to come back anytime illegally, I discussed my point of view and I told them what I was thinking, but many who have been deported have found the way to come back, they told me that it is just a matter of money. Indeed, I met some women who have been deported for more than 3 times. How do you do that I asked them, you just need money to solve that issue; there are people who live from that business, they smuggle and this can not just end overnight.

On Sunday 20th of December 2008, I heard girls talking about an additional 27 females coming in by the evening. Why so many? Where were they coming from? I was very sad to hear that news, in my mind I was saying that someone should be compassionate and not apprehend people during this period of time, it was so hard to see what was going on. Most of time women complained about their kids, they have been picked up from work, from the street, my kids were in school, my husband was at is work . . . Or the husband was also picked up and was in the men section and kids have been left alone on the street without knowing very much what happen to their parents. Women were crying, and I was going around talking an consoling. Why catching those illegal should have been made at this period of time? Family needed to be kept together, I was very sad even though I was trying to stay strong, I was broken for all those women. Before night, that day 7 new comers were brought to our unit, one of them had a cast at one foot. They were very young below 20 years of age. Why so young they adventure themselves to come to America? What can justify this courage and sacrifice? I then understood that the worst economy of development countries, the war in many countries of the world and the cartel drug war in Mexico didn't leave many choices to people. Since the beginning of 2008, almost 5300 drug related deaths in Mexico, this is a tragedy and the battle that Mexican authorities and most of South American countries are losing. Even though the Mexican state has poured 3000 in Mexico streets, the government military are confronting gangs super equipped with kalashinikov, rocket, grenades and home made bomb. This type of new war can easily destabilize the government and the population. The tranquility and the peace are at gang mercy. This somber picture of Mexico is the same for most of Central American countries which explain the great migration to the North America. Nevertheless, no government should support "drug and human exploitation". When I asked those young people the question why they risked their life to come to USA, they told me that there are organized Mafia groups who are doing business and exploiting children sexually. I was chocked, I was far to understand and at time I didn't know what to say. I then learned that those young people walked for 6 days in the bush, in the Arizona desert before they reached the border. It was so difficult to walk so long without proper shoes, without water, without food. They were exhausted, and they said that while walking you have to put in your last strength and breath otherwise the group will abandon you to die in the wilderness. During their walk, they even saw the remains of a couple man and wife and when they asked their guide what could have happened to those people, they have been told that the female couldn't walk further, she was tired and sick and she asked to stay. Her husband who has been helping and holding her for a long distance was also exhausted, he suggested to stay with her then they die together. This is macabre and curious, it seems like the smugglers knew that story; could that be the same people? It was hard for me to picture what those kids went through. Abandoned to die in the wilderness, abandoned to the votours fist; unfortunately it is that sometimes the price or the value to what the human being could be reduced. (The girl with the cast at the foot was hit by a rock thrown by one of border patrol guy) The girls also mentioned that there were more than a thousand walking from the South to USA, I was then more than chocked. How come countries are abandoning their own people? I think that each country should be able to provide to their people needs and create a stable and sustainable vital environment for the well being of their people. It is inadmissible that in this era some countries appeared to be stable and provide for their people and other countries seem to be overloaded by worst management and let their people turn their life to nomad and charity. This is also the case for many African countries which are lead by selfish, ignorant and incapable dictators who don't have much to give to their people but only hardship and misery. I sometimes think that above those states/countries we need a third power in case the inner power of local population is muzzled. There are countries that have never been capable of doing the minimum for their people or provide a viable space for their population. I sincerely think that there is a global problem here. Countries that can not provide for their people should be indexed and should be able to respond to the international community and inquisition for abusing and neglecting their people. For more than 4 decades of independency it is difficult to evaluate the progress in most of African independent countries. It is scandalous to see how the world has accepted the institutionalization of poor leadership and dependence to the exterior. We should understand that for so long, the language should have changed since, we should have been able to learn, to fail, to back up, to rise up again, restart and really take off and become independent. I consider that the migration is a plague and should be addressed without complaisance. It's a crime against humanity, we should be able to address the migration, the nomadic and wandering issue as we address the poverty issue, the AIDS issue or any other issue at global level.

People are paying fortune to come to USA or to enter Europe. Those girls paid $6000.00 to $8000.00, it really wasn't worth since they have to go back, they have sold their soul to the devil it's not working this way. Some have paid this amount and died on their way, they have been lied to without pity or any human sensitivity by the human smugglers. This is the same situation in Australia, Europe and elsewhere in the world. We have been accustom to the migration for quiet bit long time and some places there is a massive movement of population from one country to another. People are in search of happiness, of peace, of well being and survival conditions.

I caught Erika and a new friend Hannah discussing and Erika was sustaining that people coming from South America have hard time to come to America and on the other hand Hannah was sustaining that people from Africa were coming from far away and had hard time to make it to America. According to Hannah people or immigration always consider that refugee from Africa can just go back to Africa and they never think how far and expensive it is. Comparing African to Mexican she then said that Mexican are just coming from behind the house and they are coming back anytime they want. Erika objected and she said that in reality that is not true because some refugee from the South America have been dropped in the Arizona desert full of snake and they walk fro many days without food, without any drink even though they have paid a fortune to the smugglers. She also mentioned that the desert is full of human remains. I was standing by and didn't want to intervene, most of the time while people are discussing this type of things they want to pull the cover on their side. In reality, where ever you are coming from and going to new land to settle it is never easy, you can not make it on your own, unless some goodwill stand on your way and bless you.

Oh my God Christmas is in two 2 days, and I was still locked up. I didn't know how to keep going, we have all being sick. Christmas was sold on TV, there was no channel that wasn't exploiting Christmas, the shopping spree and those crazyness. I saw women crying, when I asked them what was that about, all of them mentioned their family, their kids. They missed them so much, when it was the first time to be away from your love one, it hurt so bad. Christmas is happiness, but we all have been sad to death and we couldn't comprehend this reality. That was my first Christmas out of the world, far away from home. But my friend Erika has been their for 3 years, how come? She was crying and she show me the gift bag she has got from the Detention Center since the 1st Christmas. Those bags were not empty, they were goodies, candy. Why do you still keep this Erika, I asked her. She told me with tears that she promised her kids that they were going to open them together the day she will get out of Detention Center, that day never happened Erika was deported after 3 years of detention. I never knew the real reason why she was kept so long in Detention Center, but she confide one day that her problem was like a personal fight with one of the big guy from the immigration service. She has been arrested 3 years ago and once in that strange officer office, she asked for the phone. She had called her sister and asked her to get her kids and her sister kid out of school and told them to hide. Her kids school thought to fight the immigration by going in public war on TV and . . . this is all I knew about, and the immigration was not happy with this situation. She told me she sacrifice herself for her family. I wish really she was not locked so long, she is such nice person and her kids need her. For so long in detention she was deported anyway. To help cope with the situation one of the rare officer who seem to be kind Mrs. T she told us that we were going to have a good lunch on Christmas a beef roast. That was cool and we really waited for that meal impatiently. Before lunch we hold our hands and pray to bless the food and asked the Lord to strengthen all those broken heart. We had a good lunch and tried to talk and laugh even though this didn't look like appropriate on the day where most of us had to deal with the absence from the family table. On December 25th 2008, I thought that Christmas was finally over. Yes Christmas was over, that feeling at that particular moment was the same I usually have after Christmas lunch or dinner. I always had the impression that Christmas is before the 25th of December and on the evening of 25th it is already over. The officer told us another good news for the food on the 1st of January 2009. Oh! Really I wish that those people didn't consider to offer that kind of food for new year, I wish I had the every day poor meal. When we saw the food, we started talking and saying, this is not what she told us. Indeed the food was turkey ham, I never seen that type before. It had a plastic/gum aspect and was stinky. I saw tears in many eyes, mine were also in tears. Why they were giving us that kind of food on New Year, that came to add to our pain and sadness. We throw almost everything, we couldn't eat, someone really didn't care and even if we complained, there was no way to win anything; we were the forgotten. That was not the first time.

On 12th of January 2009 I was in the sitting area and was looking at the bed behind where we have been sitting and I noticed that all bed have been occupied. I was looking at the scene and I said to myself that in case someone is in deep sleep and forget herself, she would run over and fall. Also that place was like a recreation spot where people were loud, the light was very bright; how come someone would be able to sleep there? As I was running my eyes all around, I noticed a scene that made me laughed to the point I forgot where I was. There was a woman who was well inspired to prevent a fall, she was laying down with her legs opened and her feet turned in lock on the side of the mattress. I shaked my head and thought that she was smart to do so. With that happy moment my spirit was lifted, I made a call to my friend for his birthday. Around 5 o'clock that day I thought to have some rest before dinner I went to my room and lay in my bed. As soon as my head touched the pillow, I was surprised to see that the pillow was wet, my sweater that was in the bed was also wet. I told my roommate and I asked where this water could come from? I looked up, I didn't see where the leak could come from, because my bed was in the bottom and hers was the top. Without hesitation Coco, my roommate lifted the heard of her mattress to check; what are you doing? I asked her. I am checking because I remember that I have hide a pack of milk here, I might have laid on it without paying attention. What I asked her, I wasn't made we started laughing very loud for almost 10 minutes. Coco was funny, we talked a lot and we laughed a lot but she never like to clean. Anyway, she was sorry for what happened and we just laughed at it. Indeed in detention center or in prison you have to be in survival mode, every day you have to think and think fast to how to survive. I heard my friend telling me that everyday. I think that one of the reason people should not stay too long in prison is that there they can really learn and learn the bad that is acceptable in prison but not in society. The blade is not allowed in detention center, but I saw blades on hands of women all day. Drug is not permitted, no people are doing drug in detention center, I noticed that hyper people are those who were drinking strong coffee and even tea and on top they needed just to add an acetaminophene or another drug. I was surprised when my roommate told me that she passed the rest of the drug that was prescribed by the doctor to one lady, who you could tell she was on drug. Where did she get that, no in prison they know how to make the cocktail. I told my roommate that she was not allowed to do that, she needed to watch herself, and if that person die? I told her that she will be traced, was it enough to dissuade her? I don't know but that was the practice, the stuff learned inside the detention center. We have all been hiding food in our clothes, under the mattress to have it later because we were not sure to have good food the next meal. The officer should never catch you, it was forbidden to keep food in the room. That was the rule, and in case you are unfortunate enough to get caught, you are written out. I myself did the forbidden stuff, I remember wrapping the bread 4 times in tissues and putting it under my bed. I am the one who taught Coco, we needed to survive. We needed to keep the bread, milk, fruit unless we wanted to recuperate them in the garbage. The officers once they found the food, they threw it in the garbage. No, nobody has ever gone to the garbage to look for the food, that was the little dignity we had to keep with us, to make it through. But the garbage was the final destination of the hidden food. What all of us didn't understand is that this treatment worked in case the food is coming from the detention kitchen, we were allowed to keep the food bought with our own money. The reason was to avoid mice, do you know how the mice would distinguish the food from the detention kitchen and a bowl of noodles that came from the commissary or a piece of dry sausage from the commissary?

I had true moment of laugh that day, I was sitting at the round table with a lady named Maria, she always looked shy and smiling without a word coming out of her mouth. There was a bottle of chili sauce in the middle of the table, she picked it and read loud "shake before use", then she started laughing. I asked Maria what was that about, she was delighted and said that she remember one of her young uncle who was taking a medication and it was written on the bottle "shake hard before drinking" instead of shaking the bottle, the uncle who was 11 years at that time was shaking himself, he was running hard before taking the medication without even shaking the medication. That was Maria best shot in a long time I have known her. We needed those kind of stories to shake ourselves. I laughed and felt very good. Jokes and laughs should rule in the detention center. At 9 pm I was taking my shower when I overhead a conversation between two ladies. One of them Ella must have been crackhead in her former life. She was so instable, she usually walked with her butt up, like if there was an hunter around, she was walking it and many times I saw her doing the stripper dance for her friends, holding the door in place of the pole; that dance was very dirty and too revealing. Ella was the drama queen, she liked to victimize herself. She fantaisized by saying that her Father who was Dr, was punishing her and refused to pay a bond for her. That was not true, people who knew her said that she was a pathetic lier. Then Ella was telling her friend that when she will get out she will be working for $180 per hour. Her friend then asked her, what will you be doing? Are you going to be a prostitute? Oh yes, for sure that is what she was going to do. She was obviously preparing herself to that life, the dance, the walk etc . . .

The election day will stay for ever in my memory, I was sitting in front of the TV watching CNN, John King with the magic screen, I was calm and was waiting for the results, before even Wolf or John King confirm that Obama was President, I yelled he got it, he is president. The girls were not sure yet and the asked me how did I know? I told them that I was watching the figures on the screen. When CNN announced the results, I couldn't fake it, I jumped high, very high, I yelled to release all the pressure. I was very happy, the detention center was in fire, the noise were coming from everywhere. Erika came to look for me and grabbed me by my arm, she told me that she wanted to pray, for the President and the country; we went out, it was raining and we said our prayer. Later when I called my sister in Canada, it was my 10 years old niece Rachel who picked the phone, she said "maman Jenny, did you watch TV? Obama won? I said yes I watched the TV, he won. She knows how much I was interested in the politics and election business. I then spoke to everybody, it was a celebration. On 20th of January 2009, I could paid anything to negotiate TV and watched the boss, the president Obama's inauguration. I followed and supported him since the beginning. I was so happy for him, that was the journey I started on my own alone in my apartment in Edmonton. I shared my intimacy with the politics, I was committed. Things I was listening, the words, the magnitude of the elections, I couldn't share with my fellow inmates. They never understood why I was "wasting" my time (that is what they used to say to me) watching the news, specially CNN. They asked me that question many times and I had to explain to them, but I don't think that they understood a word of what I was saying; one of the girl told me that she was even surprised that her mother in law was also watching the news specially CNN, she naively asked to know if this means that she is smart, she has a degree; I answered that could be. The girls were happy to see Obama winning, but they were not ready to follow him everywhere and every time. I had to negotiate sometimes to watch TV, they were more interested in stars life the symbol of successful story and the American dream; the success, money and fortune, the beauty and the plastic surgery . . . they even told me one day that they don't care about politicians and they don't like them. For them politicians are just doing politics and once voted they will forget them. I couldn't help I was driven by the news, the politics and for no reason I could miss that event. Oh my God, this event is the only one of this magnitude I have ever witness in my life time. The inauguration was very big and the technology rendered everything so catchy for the eyes, all those people I was thinking and praying that everything went smoothly. Indeed thinks went well and I didn't miss the moment, when the president put his hand on the bible, tears rolled on my chick . . . that was beautiful. I am one of the rare who never thought that this will never happen, but to be frank I never think of it. I know that life is a struggle and full of barrier, but I never think that it can be impossible to achieve your dream. The force that has been driven me all those years is above all and I believe that anything is possible. I never doubt that this will happen one day. I was very happy that this event could happen in my life time.

On 21st of January I was doing my hair when suddenly my Chinese roommate Coco, came to see me and told me that I seem to be friendly with the girl who was doing my breads and she asked me why that girl wasn't moving with me, then she will move out with another Chinese girl. I looked at her and decided to tell her the truth "for more than a month she has been sharing my room and she never clean" I was very upset with her and I asked her the day before to do something, to make her bed. The news was spread everywhere that we were not getting chicken that week because my room was not tidy. Many times the officer enter my room and sermon Coco and asked her to make her bed and this order was coming like after 4 or 5 warning. Too late, we were not going to have chicken that week. The next day I was surprised to see Coco cleaning the room, no this is a type of people who try to play you and tell you good things just because they want you to fill appreciated, maybe for being kind or stupid by not saying anything to them. That was not the end of my surprise, I was getting ready to sleep and I started praying when Coco entered the room and told me that our room was not a lucky room, the fong (Chinese lucky charm) was missing in the room. I said what is that stupidity, what is the "fong"? I laughed on top of my lymph and then didn't pursue the conversation since she had to run to get her laundry bag. When she came back I told her that where ever I am, in my room, in my house there is a spirit of God and no spirit can stand God spirit. I told her that I didn't need lucky charm to have good life, I was blessed even though I was in detention. I asked her what she was thinking about her friend Chinese who have been there for more than 2 years? What about their room, where was the fong? The next think I know, she left the room while I was away, it was Saturday. The only day we were allowed to walk out of the unit to go to the church if it is not for medical, immigration or to meet the judge. The Saturday when I came back from the church Coco was no longer in the room, she took all her stuff and moved with her Chinese friend. I didn't care about what ever Coco was doing, but I was somewhere surprised to see her reading Pastor Warren book "The purpose driven life" translated in Chinese, I asked her if she understood what she was reading, I told her that the things the pastor was talking about are things that I believed in. She was Buddhist, I don't know how Christians and Buddhists are related. But she allowed me time to time to pray for her and before I left the detention center she was going to the church, and I told her that Jesus and the church was my lucky charm. I loved her no matter what, she was beautiful inside and outside.

By the end of January I was so tired of everything and I started feeling very sick, sometimes I was going outside in the cold for prayer or talk with my friend Erika, talks I didn't want to share with other girls. Especially when I needed to give her advice, she was leading the prayer in the morning and had fight from everywhere. There was a group of girls who didn't like her and she was not a type of letting it go easily. I had to create time frame to help her with all my advices. I staid in the bed little bit longer that day I was seriously sick and I asked to go to see the doctor. We were like 8 of us, going out for doctor visit that day; at the medical unit we had been kept in a cold cell and have been called one by one to see the doctor. I saw the Dr. on my turn and I didn't like the way she was treating people, but I tried to be patient. My skin was reckeing and was itcthy some places, after I explained to her what I had; she checked the affected surface and mentioned that my skin had the same mark that looked to be there before. I told her that I have noticed the itchy skin and dark spot on my skin during my detention and I never had that before. She gave me the medication and she promised to give me additional medication, but mean while she excused herself and asked me to go back to the waiting room. We had to wait that everybody be consulted for us to proceed back to our unit, and during this time I was expecting that the strange Dr. will give me the rest of medication, it took quiet long time and when an officer opened the waiting room to let some girls who were done with the medical visit; I asked him to do me a favor, to go and told the Dr, to remember my medication but instead of remembering that she told the officer that she was done with me and she didn't have additional medication for me. I was very upset and through the window on the door I saw her and waived on her direction to remind her that it was me. The cell where we have been was locked, and to hear from a voice from outside you need to put certain decibels to have yourself be heard. Indeed that is what she did, she yelled in the hall way just in front of the cell where we have been, she shouted in my direction telling me to stop and she cursed. She was very loud and inside me I said what is this? In the medical section you are yelling on people? I learned in detention center the definition of who is white and who wasn't. It was a kind of weird because really I never thought that I will be discussing a topic like this, talking about races unless is to teach people how who should be acceptable of each race, how to be color blind. The girl from Fidgie told me that the white in America are the Irish, the British who came 1st during the American colonization. I was educated but that was something I really ignored and I don't know if I had to buy that explanation till indeed I check this information. And by looking at that Dr she looked like an immigrant, like the rest of us, like Mexican like whoever except a native. I felt so bad and I said to myself, oh is this mean that by being in detention center we are all crazy people and worthless? I felt very bad, and I promised that in case I will be going to the medical unit, I will chose who will consult me or there will be no consultation. No I was not going to give an opportunity to that Dr who had memory shortage by forgetting that she was also immigrant. I am glad, I never went back to the Dr. visit till the day I left the Detention Center. The girls complained about her, she was not treating them well; she was looking down on them. Comparatively to the male Dr. who have been very nice and always smiling to us, she was acting like another immigration officer. I wasn't really feeling good, I wish I was home, resting or reading. The Detention Center was packed and the girls were loud. The sleeping was 11h00, but there were still girls outside for the cleaning and entertaining the officer. The silence usually comes around 1h00 AM and at 5h00 AM we were up; and while trying to catch up with the sleep during the day, you could be surprised by an impromptu visit of the officer standing in the middle of your room telling you to make your bed or searching into your stuff to see if you are hiding food. Nevertheless I kept the bed till I felt little bit stronger and got my strength back. Since that cold, I never try to get out and play.

I got out on evening and saw Erika shooting some baskets ball outside then I run to her and I shot some baskets and enjoyed the moment. Then I said oh I never seen you playing, this is very cool. She said yes, I am shooting like my boyfriend "Michael Jordan" and I said to her "keep dreaming", I liked your boyfriend but I didn't like his divorce. Can you believe that this divorce is one of the most expensive in the World? She asked: Why, does he think that $180 millions dollar are going to replace his family, wife and kids? I don't know Erika, that is Michael business I told her, besides this I think that he still have love and admiration for his wife. I thought that the discussion was ending there and it wasn't, then Erika jumped into tearing OJ. Simpson down and said yhe I hope that he is not going to end up like OJ Simpson, a thief. I was shoked and silent, what Erika was trying to tell me, it was not relevant Michael and OJ stories are so different, I was trying to understand when suddenly she started talking about her father from Mexico and Mexicans. There is something funny about my people, she said, what funny about your people? I asked her. In my country we have people called "chillanco", they are thieves specialist. And when you recognize one by his accent, he would deny his origin and disown his people; they don't like to be identified. Up till today, I don't think that was a funny way of talking about people even though I could see that coming. I can sometimes read through people mind or project what next, I was like looking for the way to stop her putting those people down; I thought doing good by telling her that we have bad people in every society, in reality human being are alike. There is a human nature in every human being. But she kept going with her story, you know my father hate those people, he always says that I would easily forget a murderer or any other type of criminal than a thief. Her father thinks that the murder or any other criminal except a thief has balls. I said to her wait a minute Erika, it is just strange to me that your father would rather forgive a killer than a thief? Yes she said and then she threw into my face here in America those Mexicans and blacks are the big thieves. I looked at her in the way of telling her did you see that I am black? Are you insulting me? I was shut and couldn't say a word. She kept going, blacks people in America are the biggest thieves. Even if someone has money, you can see him going to seven 11 and grab food etc. without paying. I was shocked and was just listening, this observation I wanted my friend to vomit what she had inside of her, beside the preaching and the "love" she pretended showing to me. I wondered and asked myself what is this? Love, hate, destruction of someone image, confirmation of something? I didn't know why she deliberately wanted to hurt me. I knew that she was going to take some liberties, it's why since the beginning, I told her that there are bad people in every society, but she didn't get that. I was praying that the discussion end there, this was a type of discussion where most of the time is difficult to see you winning because each one would like to be right and I was not strong enough to keep discussing with my friend, sincerely if I would have had pursue it was to hurt her in return. I don't remember finishing this conversation, I run away. I didn't want to fight, I told Erika that I was catching cold, I left. I didn't know if I had to fight for blacks or Mexicans Chillancos, I left and never talk about this conversation again. But as I am writing this down few months later, I don't want to miss the opportunity of sharing some thoughts. I think that each life is the reflection of itself in the mirror, try to smile and be beautiful in front of the mirror, that is what you get when you smile at the world; try to act like angry or batman, that is what you get. The world is full of judgemental people who don't forgive any mistake and besides this we are all human being. Many ignore that it takes so little to love, to be compassionate and to be able to turn things around. I was lost somewhere in Kent (WA) a month ago while I was looking for the pastor house, and I end up in a building complex which was 15 minutes walk away from the pastor house. A lady who was working in the recreation center suggested to drive me where I was going; she left her work to help a stranger, she was white and I am black. I was not surprised and I was very grateful, but when she told me that they used to pray at the same place where we usually have Sunday service, I understood and I looked at her and I said to her, truly it takes someone who knows God, who love the world no matter what race you are to go extra miles without calculation. By the way "race" shouldn't matter if instead of "race" we just call that "human race"? I sometimes see all those color of the skin like flowers in the garden, I think that it could have been boring to have just one color of skin, imagine everything is red in your garden? What, the creator might have been out of imagination? This is the reason why I am trying to do good to people and get along. During this writing, I was walking downtown Seattle when I met a Big white guy, a traveler with a suitcase. He asked me where was the tunnel, since I was going in the same direction I told him to walk with me. I saw him hesitating, I insisted and I told him that I was going in the same direction, somewhere I see him staying little bit behind; he looked scared. I walked him to the tunnel and I even told him what bus to catch to the airport. Do we have to do those simple things only to our own people? In any community you have the good and the bad, but one thing sure more there will be good, more there will be the light in people life, the darkness will concede and go away. People are fighting sometimes over nothing, and I wish that everyday we can have the reflection of what we do, be able to look in the mirror and feel proud and complete. It only takes love and good will to change thinks around.

After many months spent in detention center, I was getting nervous as everybody and was praying to get out. That was not a place to be, I don't wish anyone to be locked up. But somehow even good people can end up in detention center, but on the other hand some wish to be locked for weird reasons, foolish choices. I couldn't believe my eyes while watching TV, I saw a big guy 6 foot tall, who was brought by is mom on Steve Wilkos show. His mom was complaining about her son's behavior. This poor single mom did really what all parents have been called to do. She raised this big guy, she put him in school, put clothes on is back and paid for college. As if it was not enough, the next thing she realized is that he turned himself to be a lazy monster who threatened his mom, and shocked her. I couldn't believe what came out of his mouth, I quote "I like prison because in prison you have free meal, you have TV" he should have added that you don't work, you don't pay your rent, you don't pay your bills. I was very shocked and asked myself, if is it worth to go to prison for TV all day or to avoid to pay rent and bills? How come in the world someone can trade his freedom for so cheap? I will never think to sell my freedom unless I am foolish. Anyway people should know that none of us is above the law. Just don't mess with the law, I told the girls in the detention center that they should not mess with the law, the law is above all and none of us is presumed to ignore the law. Sometimes those who are in charge of enforcing the law can make mistakes and you walk out, but remember the law by itself is right, is justice. This doesn't exclude it is good interpretation, it is there that you may see a charitable hand, someone understanding, compassionate and loving giving you a 2nd chance.

After I left the Detention Center, I kept contact with some few friends I met there. Time to time I could talk to Emma who was already in Mexico. Emma is a young Mexican who is 19 years old and was deported since she was caught up in prostitution. She lived in California since she was 2 years old, but growing up she made a bad choice. As soon as she got of high school, she chose to live on the street, she never wanted to go in detail of her past life; but she had mentioned one time that a cop put her on the street. She was also on drug. One day the luck was not on their side and both of them were busted and arrested, but Emma never told the full story. While in detention, she was fighting everyday with girls and officers, it was easy to notice that she was coming from where there was no rule. One of the rule created by people on the street is never listen or respect people. After 5 months in detention, Emma was still living like on the street. It was very hard for her to understand the rules, the discipline. Then I don't know how it started but she decided one day that she wanted to change, she wanted to learn about God. She spoke to Erika and she started really investing her time in reading scriptures and sharing the words. God works in mysterious ways and he is the only capable of changing and making it where it seems impossible. Then she became more receptive, and trying every day to stay out of trouble. This change was not coming so easy, time to time you could found Emma acting like the old Emma. She could do sneaky stuff and think that she could go away. She appreciated me and liked to get advice from me, what I did without reserve. I wanted her to change for her own sake. She had a lot to learn, like how to talk to people, what to say to people, how to care about what she was doing and what she was saying. She didn't give dime of who was who . . . I am the double of Emma age, but sometimes even though she was trying to be nice with me, she was capable of dropping a bomb. It was very difficult to ask Emma to be respectful. As I am writing this I just remember that she seems even to be cold to my taste, I mean she wasn't showing emotion at all and I couldn't tell that she loves people. She didn't know what love is, by being on the street so young, by giving her body to strangers, no she said that "she hated herself" she wasn't love and she didn't know what love is. I understood that she was admiring me and also wanted to learn from me, but I sometimes lost my patience by seeing how impolite Emma could be. The first fight I had with her was about the "chicken". About the chicken? Yes it was, well I didn't like the food in detention center. I was telling the girl that if they need to eat chicken, they needed to pray to have it and another prayer was "pray for an important visitor" the heavyweight visitor who usually bring the camera crew with them. All of us were complaining about that food, I heard many times girls saying that it wasn't the food they could even give to their "dog". As everybody I was talking about the food even Emma herself. But I was shocked that Emma was trying to be smart and she said something really I didn't appreciate. We have been 2 weeks without chicken, and that day they served the chicken. Emma was commenting and making jokes and was saying that she hope "the chicken could make me happy". I looked at her and I said "what?" she repeated and I was very mad and I let her know that I wasn't going to die if I don't have chicken. Then she said that I was complaining about food everyday and I should know that there are some people who don't have even the minimum we had. Somewhere I think that makes sense, really on the street Emma didn't have much and being on drug she wasn't even eating. But somewhere as I am remembering that day, I was thinking at the quality of what people usually give, the quality of the donation, the free gift you don't price. All my life I have seen many people who are giving only what they don't need or the excess. I felt like Emma was telling to someone who is poor to just accept whatever rotten food because he doesn't even have the minimum. In my mind I pictured a gift, I chose for someone who don't have, I vision a quality of what we give to other, will I going to give to him/her my old shoes just because he can not even buy any new for himself? Should I give rotten food to a homeless because where he is he can not provide for himself? Giving is a grace, 2 Corinthians 8:7 says "therefore, as ye abound in every thing, in faith, and utterance, and knowledge, and in all diligence, and in your love to us, see that ye abound in this grace also". How then do we give to people and in fortiori to God? In Malachi 1:1-14: God refused to receive Israel's offerings.

They were bringing him their defective animals, in Malachi 1:7-8 God said to Israel: Ye offer polluted bread upon mine altar; and ye say, wherein have we polluted thee? In that ye say, the table of the Lord is contemptible. And if ye offer the blind for sacrifice, is it not evil? And if ye offer the lame and sick, is it not evil? Offer it now unto thy governor; will he be pleased with thee, or accept thy person? Said the Lord of hosts. The Lord was not happy with the sick animal that were offered into sacrifice to him, the Governor neither will be happy and nor the people. That was my point, but Emma couldn't get that.

I was very shocked and I left the table. It wasn't always easy to talk to Emma, she had her idea of life and most of the time it was difficult for her to be open to new information. Most of the time we had chicken, one of the girl who had a chance to get out of the Unit because of family visit could come and tell us that "hey girls, there are camera outside I am sure we are getting chicken on the menu". The food was very bad, I can rate it 2 to 10. Everyday the food was thrown, because it was indigest or sometimes not well cooked or sometimes it was mixed the way it shouldn't be. Who have ever created bean/potatoes receipe? This is disgusting. To not starve, we had an ersatz "the commissary", this fuck commissary was for the immigration "supply" or . . . really I don't know how he end up doing business with the Detention Center. All of us were placing how order for food, telephone cards or toilette products twice a week. Most of us were buying tortilla, noodles soup that many don't even eat at home, cheap cookies, and cheap whatever. Somewhere we were like, that food was not quality food, but someone wanted to promote the commissary business. I remember one time I almost cry on week end because I didn't get my money on time and since we were used to have bad food on week end, I was expected to order food from commissary, unfortunately since I didn't have money I was starving and very upset. Then Erika was looking at me and she always do little miracle, few minutes later she brought me a pack of noodles that saved my day.

Emma left the detention center a month earlier than me. Around the time she left, we made peace and we tried to get along till she left for Mexico. It was emotional, but she was still like cold. I will never know what was going true her mind. Emma was though as the life on the street. After I got out of the detention, we talked few times on the phone, and she seems like normal person. She told me that she decided to stick to the faith and work for the Lord Jesus and also she was going back to school. I was happy for her and encourage her to keep her dreams alive. After I have received few peaceful calls from Emma, it was like the lion was sleeping, because I really don't know how we started discussing again, and getting hard on each other. I couldn't believe that I am in USA and Emma is in Mexico and we had a fight over the President Obama Health Care on the phone. The fight started slowly and in the way I couldn't avoid it. Emma is sneaky and always knows how to get on people nerves. The 1st subject of fight is that on one side Emma who is all Mexican and who lives outside USA was interested in the President Obama business and health care, on the other hand I am foreigner refugee in USA. I don't know how ones can picture this, but this happened. Emma started first to tell me that she knows how much I like politics and she knows that I am well informed, but she wanted to know if I knew that the President Obama was socialist (?). I was surprised and I asked her where she got that information, Emma will tell me that she read that on internet, and the news is everywhere. Then I told her that is good to read stuff on internet and also watch the news and listen to the debate. She was like no, Jenny what I am telling you is true . . . I said to Emma there is no way that America can turn socialist because of President Obama, this country has been founded on capitalism since 1800, there is no way to change the direction at 180 degrees. Then I asked her if she knew what socialist means, she didn't know what it is and I took the dictionary and I read the definition to her. I thought she understood and we had to close the discussion there, but she kept pushing and insisting that there were stuff on internet that she thought they are true. To shut Emma down and cut her short, I said : Eh Emma, by listening to you it sound like I am talking to a rich Republican and beside this you are not American, you are outside of USA and I am not American neither, so why are we fighting? All that sound very stupid and I pulled the last strength to shut her down and I told her we are going to talk another day. Frankly I wasn't getting anything about healthcare debate, I didn't know anything about this business and seeing Emma who still have parents in USA, who are working under the table trying to discuss a subject she doesn't get was sad, she wasn't even thinking about her own parents. All this was ridiculous, I was upset against myself, for letting Emma took over my emotion and mood. A week later, I was watching the news and I saw some fight about healthcare, I started laughing by myself in my apartment, I just see how stupid it was that I gave Emma so much time to discuss and fight over a subject that wasn't concerning me. Oh it wasn't over, Emma called two weeks later we spoke about things and things then politely she said: "Jenny I remember that the last time we spoke, you got upset about my question regarding Obama and healthcare business, but this time there is a lot and I am just asking you to check this website . . . I don't remember which one was it, I wasn't interested and I told her: Emma, stop that I really don't want to discuss that matter, she kept pushing insisting, I said no Emma I am not going to read those chiffon, I watch the news and it's enough for me. Then I told Emma, let me tell you something that you might not know, even though I am not American I have supported Obama since the beginning of the campaign, I think that he is very intelligent and if you want, you can check with my friend in Canada. I told them all that he was going to be president, this means that if I would have had a chance to vote, I would have vote for him and support him true all his presidential years, so it doesn't sound right for me to browse any cheap website on internet and taking all they are saying and put that on Obama credit; she pushed the button and at last I said this : Emma I see that you are not happy with Obama, but unfortunately you are Mexican and you live outside USA, do you get that and who care? I am not myself an American. Before I hang up I added that if it happen that you have a chance to vote, please wait the end of Obama term then you will chose your candidate. Oh I am praying that Emma will give me peace. You see how come sometimes we are proved, and I just remember this young man who was upset when I told him to commit himself into God hands and he shut me down telling me that there are 3 things you should never discuss about: politics, religious, sports. Because those 3 things always separate people. Yeh he might have been right, but the only thing I would never keep silent is to talk about Jesus. Truly I would appreciate keep talking about the Lord Jesus with Emma, we are on common ground on this topic. But talking politics, with Emma this is a subject that I master more than she is, then since she doesn't even acknowledge that she doesn't know and she is pretending, this is very difficult for us to sustain an healthy conversation on politics. I decided to firmly avoid that next time I will have a chance to talk to her. Guess what, Emma didn't give me much time to think, she already sent me an email asking for forgiveness, ah Emma: "Hello my sister Jenny, How are you today? I hope your life been good & I trust it is because you have Jesus in your heart. My sister I know last time we talked we had different opinoins but thats okay because we are daughters ot The Lord and we have his love, I remebered 1 corinthians chapter 13 verses 4-7 that we are sisters in Christ and I love you in Jesus. So how have you been? whats new? have you talked to Erica? Well I wanted to remind you that I have much respect for you, and I understand how you feel but dont worry we will never talk about the subject again I dont want to upset you because I care about you. I will not let the enemy laugh at us we will laugh at him! Amen my sister! I apologise to you Jenny forgive me. I missed you and wanted to write to you to say hi. I praise The Lord for transforming my life. Well may The Lord Bless You GreatlyKeep in touch and God bless you. Emma » I still love Emma, there was no reason not to forgive, she is just young and want to learn.

A week before I left the detention center, I had a new roommate, a very sweet girl from Europe, gosh I forgot her name? How come, how could I? She was such a nice and sweet person. I felt so good having her with me and sharing those last moments with her. She told me that she got registered in a school here in US and she got a visa, but she was arrested at the airport. I asked her what did they retain against her, she said that they said that she had a fake visa. Again another 2 years visa, I knew deep inside me that was a though case. And she was told that she was going to be sent back home. She was coming from Eastern Europe, from one of those European poor country. She was coming from a poor family and she has paid $2000 for the visa. Just by hearing the amount she paid, I knew that was fake. There are people in this world who don't care, they are taking advantage of people who even don't have the minimum to survive; they saved every penny to fulfill their dream and in one turn of evil hand, everything is gone is turned dust. It was sad since she also dreamed of American dream and was hoping to meet her fiancé at the same time, she was very sad and sometimes crying. No matter how life could be hard, I always find the way to get out of people the happiness, the next thing I can remember, we were laughing like crazy, we were so loud that some women passing by even stopped at our door, what is going on here they have been asking. They were so curious, but we didn't pay attention them, we were still laughing for a long time. My roommate was telling me how she has been checked at the airport, detail scrutiny. And she said, I could not believe that those officers were picking my pants one by one counting them and then I heard one saying that these are pretty lingerie, she might be a prostitute! Oh no Lord, he didn't. Instead of being sad feeling for her or I really don't know, I just started laughing and she was laughing with me, that was it. As usual I supported her with my advices. When I left, she looked so lonely and sad, I hope she went back home quickly.

CHAPITRE III

FREEDOM AT LAST

I have been in detention for 5 months and I don't know how I made it, and never want to imagine what Erika, Rahel, Elena endured for staying locked up so long 1 year, 2 year, 3 year? Anyway God is merciful. I couldn't afford to pay a lawyer and by chance God provided one, no two for free. No way is that true? Yes it was true after I have spent a fortune in Canada paying lawyers, I finally had lawyers from heaven who I didn't need to pay. Very good people and helpful, I couldn't believe how lucky I was after all my past misery. I then told the girls that I had the faith that the day I will go to court, that will be my 1st and last and I will get out. Most of them were surprised to see me so confident, but some who had faith knew that was possible, we prayed for many who got released, we kept believing that was also possible for me to get out. I had two preliminary hearing where my lawyers just presented my case and requested that my hearing be postponed to the 2nd of March 2008, I knew that was going to be my last day in detention. I felt like my mission wouldn't have been complete if I didn't have the last opportunity to talk to Erika since she was like a leader, a person who was helping women to cop with the detention life. She needed advices and guidelines. Also I felt like talking to one officer who was so mean to Mexicans and of course to the rest of people. I have tried many time to speak to this officer, and told her that I felt like talking to her because of the way she was treated detainees. She was a young officer but somewhere it was like she was force to come to work or somewhere she was delegated in a mission to make Mexicans life miserable and also our life miserable. I will call her Ms. Terror, every single day this lady was at work, you could listen like a dog barking, don't do that, do not touch each other, this was difficult specially when some of us were leaving and she was like don't hug . . . I don't want to see walking by the rooms, don't look inside someone room. And then the list of forbidden was long. Sometimes it was like she dreamed of you she can come in fury in your room and start checking your stuff to find is you are hiding food or you have more clothes than allowed (1 uniform, 1 sweater, 2 paires of pants, 2 sports bras). I observed her for many months but somewhere I said to myself that I need to talk to her for her own good and for the good of people I was leaving behind. Somewhere the girls had enough of her, they reported on her just few weeks before I left. We have been getting hand soap from the Detention Center since I have been there and most of us instead of spending money that we didn't have buying soap from the Mafiosi commissary, we content ourselves with that little. One Saturday, that Ms. Terror was on duty, I was sitting at our habitual table when I overheard loud voices from girls and her. I walked close by, the girls were saying that they didn't understand why she was not giving them soap, that evening and they didn't have anything for the shower. She was yelling on them and saying that she doesn't care and the rules have changed no more soap from now on you need to buy your own soap (?). I think that even in prison people we still at least have rights to be treated as human being and with consideration. I was standing there like trying to say something, no I couldn't the girls were looking at me, and since I have been a peacemaker for all and always tried to be kind with both parties, the officers on one hand and the girls on the other hand, I didn't see how to help with the peace at that time. The tension was very high, she chased the girls away from her desk. Somewhere I say the "girls", they are not regular girls; they are mothers, spouses, responsible.

I avoided to talk to her that evening, and when she got replaced everybody reported to the next and they wrote a complaint note to the Lieutenant, the guy responsible of the detention business. The women were very upset, the fight was so imminent. If that was outside, for sure they would have fight with this officer. I don't know why she was always insensitive, she even threw at me later that she doesn't care, she doesn't like Mexicans. The girls, Erika and the rest of the group put this officer in prayer, we were very concern because since the incident the detainees were showing her that they didn't care about her neither. At the end of her shift, the women were praising and shouting for the new officer, and when Ms. Terror comes for her shift, all I am saying all detainees ignore her and stay quiet. They mentioned many times that they hated her. We praid for the Lord to fulfill this officer with love and compassion and also for everyone to live in harmony and peace in the Detention Center. Nevertheless, someone reported to us that the officer has been laughing at us, saying that we looked like magicians. I was shocked and I didn't blame her, she was immature and ignorant. So why wasn't she asking questions about our prayers? Talking prayers, many believed that there was a power behind what we have been doing because most of those who praid with us have been released. Then it was funny to see someone coming to us and asking a prayer, like someone who is at Dr. consultation asking for prescription. The weekend before my court day, I had a little chance to be close to the officer Ms. Terror, and I told her that I wanted to speak to her. She told me that she was going to talk to me later. But she avoided me that Saturday and we didn't talk. On Sunday, she was like playing me again by promising but every time I was going to her, she was like I am busy . . . somewhere I caught her while sitting at her desk and I told her that she needed to have compassion for the women in Detention Center, she didn't give me a chance to finish what I wanted to say, she shout at me "no I don't want to hear that, no religion things" I was standing there confused and not understanding why she was so careless and rude. I wasn't talking about religion, I was talking about people. Why she accepted to work in people environment and she doesn't like people? I insisted, then she raised her voice telling me "I don't want to hear anything" Nevertheless I found the strength, the way to get out of my mouth "you know what sometimes it takes love and kindness to change things around you". She got upset, at that point I didn't care very much, I did what I had to do. Mission accomplished, I said to myself. Then I told her smiling, look at me very well because this is the last day we are going to meet. She said to me "you have been saying that a long time ago and you still here". I smiled and left her sitting at her desk. Indeed that was the last day I was going to see her.

Before I appear in court, I put everything into God hands, my friends took the matter has their own. The day of my hearing I commit myself into God hands and during the hearing, I could see the effect of our prayer, I could feel the presence of God power. I answered to all questions, and before the prosecutor got through all the questions, a decision to grant me asylum was made. I didn't fight at all, as we asked in our prayer, on the cross Jesus won all my battles. I was even amazed to see that the spirit of the Lord brought the fight between the Judge and the prosecutor. I couldn't believe my eyes, after 7 years of struggle, it was finally over. I am getting out! I couldn't believe my ears. Did I hear well? No, not till the judge said "congratulations you are welcome to USA". Only 5 months of sacrifice and I made it? I was happy, and free at last; I hug my lawyers and thanked them, they were sent by the Lord. While going back to my Unit I jumped in the hallway, I yelled "yes, thank you Jesus". It seems like many officers have been waiting for the news, many heard me and some even said that they were not surprised. I understood then why my life in Detention didn't put pressure on me, I was not feeling the pain very much. I was one of the strongest, and most of them were coming to me for help. I was in mission and I still had unfinished business with Erika, she needed advices. Upon my return to the unit, I had a surprise of my life, from scratch my friends had prepared a king dinner. No that was not the rotten food from the Detention, that was the food they have paid for them, they made something for me "CHAO MIN" etc . . . I was very happy and grateful. Also I was surprised by the art craft that Erika had made patiently from papers she made a vase, she made flowers and from soap and coffee she offered me a page of the bible with holly words. For those art craft we even had the fight one day, because she told me to never go to her room or stop by at the time she was doing the project, she wanted that to be a surprise; I ignored that and she got very upset. Finally I was relieved and I was visioning my life outside, life of freedom. From the little recreation court of the detention we could see a portion of the sky, listen to birds songs without seeing them. I was free at last, I will be seeing a limitless sky, I will walk on the grass, I will put my feet on the ground etc . . . all crazy stuff were crossing my mind. I talked to my friends that evening and encourage them, advise them for the last time and I told them that I will never forget them and will keep contact. Before I left, my biggest mission was to talk to Erika and comfort her. She was so down and she told me that was it, she would never get out for prayer anymore, she will be staying in her room, she doesn't have friends in the detention center, during lunch she will be sitting at certain table . . . A very long list of limitations to what she was really supposed to do. I told her to keep being patient and loving for the women in the detention center and also as she was a leader she shouldn't chose only does who liked her or talk only to those people, I asked not to have a preference and she had to accept that people are different and love them as they are and still she could create opportunity of teaching the words and help the detainees to cope with the hardship of the detention. She maintained her position and at the end I prayed for her and I told her that everything is fine, I did my part and I was asking the Lord to do his part. And I add that if I wasn't strong enough to convince you, Jesus will do the rest, that was my last deep and spiritual conversation with her. I was very sad leaving Erika behind even though sometimes she was fighting me, I loved her and still love her like a sister. It was hard to see that she was a victim of an unjust system. I was wandering why someone couldn't look into her case and considered that she was enough punished and give her a 2nd chance? I was thinking that I will be going the next day, but it didn't happen. I had to spend one more day, in detention again? At that point I didn't mind, they didn't have a reason to keep me there longer than it should be. I chat a little bit with some friends on the 4th of March, I collected few addresses and then I was sitting there getting bored and wandering about when I would finally get out. I went back to my room and took a nap, I heard my name called, the officer was calling me. I stood and I saw a bunch of women coming to my room to say good by, they were running; I was overwhelmed. The girls were running to me, I heard again the officer calling and saying "hurry up, no time to waste", then a voice among the girls said "hurry up before they change their mind" I laughed from the bottom of my lymph, no not this time. I put on the uniform, it was the last time I was putting it on. I grabbed my papers and said good bye to who ever was there. It was sad, they were crying and they asked that I remember them. No I didn't forget those women, I will never forget the detention center, it has become one chapter of my life. I spoke to many after I left the detention center. But I later contacted those who left, unfortunately most of them had the telephone cut. I stopped by the checking/checkout front desk and filled up some papers before I left. There was something I couldn't sense and that I will never cope with, I was sitting there and watching new detainees coming in, they were chained; I was ashamed, I was feeling bad and frankly when it could happened that my eyes had seen a someone chained, I couldn't looked at him twice. It was very hard for me and it seems like I will never cope with that. I retrieved my stuff, I switched the uniform to my clothes and OUF! the fresh air from outside, I felt something I will never be able to explain, the sky was beautiful, I saw cars, people wearing different clothes than uniform, I saw life.

Finally God has remembered me, I still remember the 1st time I enter USA, 20 years ago, very ambitious. I was dreaming high! I wanted to go to university and go for a master. Unfortunately my dream was bigger than my pocket, I didn't even know where to start. I wasn't speaking English, I didn't know anyone. Little money in my wallet and a saving from my pension fund of 5 years at UNICEF, was not enough. I spent 2 months studying English summer course in a very expensive school, quickly I run out of money. Nevertheless I was still hopping to pull the magic with little money that was left. From Africa, what we knew of USA was America the great, America the best and powerful, where help was pouring and running on the street, America of big cars, big houses and so . . . I tried to look around and check the reality and see if someone could help. Somewhere I tried some contacts, it was a dead end. Indeed the reality check was harder than expected. Even in America people suffer, there are homeless. People work for their money . . . It was not just the way many think about that, many imagine that it's a paradise; the reality was very different. I tried to be strong, not till I met a homeless. I was scared to the point I cried and feared that I will end up being on the street if I don't have any help. At that point I had only one alternative, sleep on the street and live hard or go back to Africa and see others opportunities. In the mix I sold some of my jewelry for little to survive. I started sleeping from house to house. I still remembered this African guy who likely was coming from a good family but end up in a relation with someone with whom he lived like in a zoo. What in the world was that filthy house above a restaurant in the middle of San Francisco Cole Street? I couldn't believe my eyes that people just neglect themselves to the point they don't smell stinky odor, they don't see the mess. Truly this African brother was a kind of lost, I guess that time he couldn't pursue is schooling because of lack of finances or he didn't have his papers in order. It also might be that he was married to this girl to have a chance of getting his residence. I remember that in nineties many African had sent their kids to America, thinking that Uncle Sam would do the magic trick to help. I called that "suicidal". Most of those people didn't know what is American reality. I know that African people are hustlers, people survive in Africa when other live and enjoy their life in the rest of the world, but in America you learn it the hard way; you might make it or not. I got lucky that somebody else tried to help me for a short period of time. A girl from France, who didn't have very much and didn't have her papers neither. I bought a sleeping bag and shared her room. San Francisco in 1991, was characterized by the roommate connection. Marie had to tell stories to the people in the house, to keep helping me with a shelter. She has been fought. She tried, she was nice, but without money or power to keep me over. She helped me sell my jewelry in downtown San Francisco where I lost 2/3 of their value. I needed to survive, I didn't care. I tried desperately to find a job, any job except for one. I have called a number that I saw in the newspaper and I asked the guy who was on the phone about the job, he asked me if I could serve in "bikini", I said what? Marie grabbed the telephone from my hand and asked the question to know what was about. The answer came out like a slap in Mary face, what kind of business is that serving in bikini? She was shouting, she cursed the guy and then hang up. I was running, chasing the winds, looking for help without even being conscious that God was watching and his hand was upon me. I have learned 20 years later to know his true face, to listen to him and to trust him. I can now understand things that are happening in my life. 20 years ago I couldn't tell how God operates, I didn't have those spiritual eyes, I now believe that there is no hazard concerning my life. I am in God plan, he knows me even before I born (?). There is no lucky but God plan. Somewhere I wish I knew God secret, I wish I heard his voice before it is too late. Indeed my choices, my decisions making would have been different if I would have known then. Through connections I finally met someone who later became like a sister for me. I was introduced to Deborah Bryant, a very nice American lady with a big heart. Deborah spoke to her husband about me and the next thing I knew, I moved with them. I was very happy to have a roof on my head and to have food; in Deborah beautiful house where I had my own bed room an the freedom of cooking what ever I needed or doing what ever I needed, there was no need for me to hide from roommates who would walk in and ask "who is this"? Deborah house was beautiful, clean, peaceful, everything you ever dream of. I didn't even notice that her husband was sick, till two of my friends from school passed by, they mentioned to me at the time they were living the house that Deborah husband was sick. I asked them how they knew that, they told me that they just looked at him and they knew. Deborah husband was suffering from AIDS, I didn't know that. 2 days later Deborah asked to talk to me, she opened to me and told me what I already knew. Her husband was indeed sick and she wasn't. That was grace she mentioned and she told me what happened few years ago in her marriage. She confided that few years ago while in Africa her husband was seeing other women, she was betrayed. Then one day she dreamed that her husband life was going to be shattered if he didn't change his life. He didn't even believe that and somewhere it was too late to adjust and take back the disease. They found out about aid when they came back from Africa during pregnancy exam, unfortunately it was too late, few months after the diagnosis her husband got sick, he was on strong medication at the time I met them. The medication were very strong, his stomach was upset and couldn't handle the medication; he was throwing, refusing to eat and losing a lot of weight. He kept going to work because for him that was the only think that was helping him to keep going. I tried my best to help them cope, I was very sad and compassionate for them. In 1991, AIDS was ravaging life, even though Deborah husband was sick, she never acted like someone who wanted revenge, she was full of love and compassion for her husband, I couldn't believe my eyes. This was bitter sweet, because her husband was dying, but on the other hand I learned a true love lesson, love at first and from the heart; she forgave him. She was caring for her husband in such way, I said to myself what happen then and why? Some mornings I could see Deborah's husband sitting in the kitchen looking at the medication and having difficulties to put them into his mouth, he told me one day that he couldn't keep taking those medication, they were hurting him instead of healing him. I was looking at him without a word and anytime I was by myself I was praying for him, and what was interesting is that every times I could pray for him, the next day he was like full of life and was doing stuff around the house or washing dishes, I was like oh it's working. But I didn't know how to sustain a faithful prayer and cast out the disease, I was too young and ignorant of how to handle a healing prayer. But anyway I was happy to see Deborah's husband smiling, looking strong the next day after I prayed. We shared some very good time going sometimes to the restaurant, and I appreciated those quality times with my friends, they were working all day and I was pleased to be with them and just talk and learn to know them. Besides caring for her husband Deborah was caring for me, she was like a sister, she was very concern that I was like staying without money. She advised me to go back to Africa and maybe I would have better opportunity. I finally decided to leave my friend around Christmas, it was cold and I was not planning to stay longer and start spending on winter clothes. The decision to go back was like a knife through my throat, even though I knew how difficult it was, I was like I wanted to try, I wanted to hustle. I have been there, I can easily understand all those immigrants and their sacrifice. I was thinking at my family and I wanted to sacrifice myself for them at any price. But since I didn't even know how to start, where to start I had to let go. A day before I went back to Africa, Deborah and her husband took me to one of the best restaurant in San Francisco at the Fisherman Warf for a dinner. The restaurant was very big and packed, it was a sea food restaurant. We ordered our sea food dish, and had fun when I was trying to grab (coquille), and it was slipping and falling luckily into the plate. I am saying luckily because sometimes they can fly land on someone head. I couldn't grab it and I just didn't eat it. I ate the easy stuff like shrimps, that was my last meal with my friends. We talked a lot, and I refused to think that I was not going to see Kurt anymore. The idea didn't cross my mind that night. My flight was early in the morning, they called the shuttle and helped me to get my stuff out. We said a prayer and I hug them to say good bye, that was my hardest separation ever. I don't know why, I started crying before even I hug them; I don't know how to explain this my eyes were pouring from that moment to the time I arrived home in Africa. I was crying for almost 3 days, just by thinking at them, even when I was telling people back home my story and talking about Deborah and husband I couldn't stop crying. As I still remember that today, I wander maybe I had a feeling that was the last time I was seeing Kurt, Deborah husband. I went back home and tried to reorganize my life, in May 1992, I had a message from Deborah that was sent through the Bahai Center in Israel to my attention. I was like what message is that, I was anxious and really at first I wasn't expecting that this message just after 6 months I have left Deborah and Kurt, I will be learning that Kurt passed away. I cried, I sent my condolences to Deborah and what next? Truly life is something. I will always cherish the good time we had together, and will always remember Kurt.

This has been almost 20 years ago, when I was dreaming to come to America and restart a new life. I didn't make it then, 20 years have passed and I forgot that. The distraction, the life maintenance made me forgot what I asked for. I forgot what I asked God 20 years earlier, but it seems like he never forget. Instead of letting me stay in Canada, he brought me back to USA; he has a purpose for me I believe that. 20 years it is a long time, I have been looking for an opportunity, I have been looking for a push, for someone to help to push the heavy door standing on my way, I was looking for the light to shine into my life. The day I got out of the detention, I went straight to my computer, I had 600 mails, from the Obama campaign and all my correspondents. I was happy and tried to go through all that, suddenly somewhere something caught my attention, my husband or my ex sent me an email? It has been more than five years I didn't hear from him, oh he still alive? I was very excited and curious to know what lies he was going to say again, but it was a relief, the lawyer wanted my address, then he could send me the divorce papers. Oh such a relief, God made it for me, there was no fights neither cries; twice I had a revelation that the ex was not coming to Canada or after me even though we planed that in the past. Things have changed, he then asked for divorce. I knew he was never going to come, I trusted those visions even though people I spoke to didn't believe.

It might have been that I have been looking in the wrong direction. Sometimes I cried, I have seen injustice everywhere and sometimes life appear to be like a jungle. I was telling to myself, Jenny you have to be strong, you have to stand strong and for sure one day you are going to make it. I couldn't vision how it was going to happen but deep inside me there was a strength that really carry me through all these years long and put so much joy into me. I live a life of happiness and real joy, I always bless and always be happy to see the happiness in other. This attitude has been weird for many, who most of the time asked me "why are you always happy"? Even when I am hurt I still have the joy within me. In detention center, my friends were asking "why are you happy every time someone got released? I sound really stupid because I was like taking part of someone life, someone who according to the girls was more blessed than I was. No, every time I am happy for someone, every time I am blessing someone I am scoring for my own blessings.

Many tried to block me, tried to block my sun. Did I say my sun? It is amazing, that while writing these lines I opened the journal that my Team Lead Patricia Peterson offered me in souvenir before I left Edmonton, she wrote these words:

September 25th, 2008

Dear Jeanne,

> How sad I am feeling to see you leave Edmonton, and my team at Sunlife! God willing for a short time.
> I wanted you to have a book to journal your thoughts as you begin this next journey of your life.
> Like a sunflower that always turns is face to the sun, keep your eyes and heart and soul turned to the SON. TRISH.

This is amazing that I just found these words of blessings from TRISH, I miss her and all the gang of Sunlife Edmonton. Indeed I like roses, I also like sunflower but the sunflower brighten my life. No matter what, I always believed that there will be a breakthrough. Many on my way blocked me trying to tell me that I needed to give more, I always give more and used for someone else interest. I know that the time will come where all that have been stolen from me, will be paid back. I refused to do vengeance, God will revenge me instead. After 20 years I understand that I would rather count in God who possessed everything than in a man. Everything is vanity and shall pass. Most of successful people think that they made it on their own, some call "blessings" "lucky", no there is no hazard. Pastor "RICK WARREN" in the Purpose Driven Life Stated: "There's a Grand Designer behind everything. Your life is not a result of random chance, fate, or luck. There is a master plan. History is His story. God is pulling the strings. We make mistakes, but God never does, God can not make mistake because he is God. God's plan for your life involves all that happens to you; including your mistakes, your sins, and your hurts. It includes illness, debts, disasters, divorce, and death o loved ones. God can bring good out of the worst evil. He did at Calvary".

As I am reaching the shinning moment of my life, I feel very blessed and amazed to see how long it can take to get the answer, how strong we need to be, how long we sometimes need to be patient.

FOR OUR LIGHT AND MOMENTARY TROUBLES ARE
ACHIEVING FOR US AN ETERNAL GLORY THAT FAR
OUTWEIGHS THEM ALL
2 Corinthians 4:17

AND WE KNOW THAT IN ALL THINGS GOD WORKS FOR
THE GOOD OF THOSE WHO LOVE HIM, WHO HAVE BEEN
CALLED ACCORDING TO HIS PURPOSE.
Romans 8:28